My Brother, My Keeper

by
Phil Cooke

My Brother, My Keeper

www.mybrothermykeeper.com

Copyright © 2008 by Phil Cooke

Library of Congress
Cataloging in Publication Data

ISBN 978-0-6152-3221-8

Manufactured in The United States of America by
CEI Publishing
2954 Timber Wood Way
Oak Hill, VA 20171

My Brother, My Keeper
The Biography of J. P. Blase Cooke
A Story of Hard Work, Success, and a
Valiant Fight to Beat Cancer

Dedication and Acknowledgments

This book is dedicated to our Mom and Dad. Thanks for all your sacrifices and for helping to bring Blase home to you.

There are so many people to thank for making this book possible. First and foremost, this book could not have happened without the tremendous support from Blase's long-time executive assistant and friend, Joani Van Tuyl. She was there from the beginning, providing me whatever information I needed, from email lists, to Blase's personal calendars, his medical records, his *Thoughts for the Day*, and more importantly, her continued encouragement to make this happen. I also want to acknowledge Chandler Vicchio and Eric Mueck from Publish Today, a Baltimore-based book publisher, who provided tremendous support and guidance in getting this book published.

Speaking of encouragement, my love and thanks go out to my beautiful wife and best friend, Wanda, who has always been my constant source of love and inspiration throughout our journey in life. To our three very wonderful and talented children, Nicol, Matt and Megan, who provided their love and support on a daily basis, and continue to do so. They were my first editors and critics who helped shape this story. My children also developed our website www.mybrothermykeeper.com, which I hope you will visit.

A number of friends and family who knew Blase well were kind enough to read draft versions of the book, and I am extremely grateful to all of them for their comments and feedback. However, I would like to acknowledge three people, two of whom never knew Blase personally, but were kind enough to review the book: Bob Neil, a great friend and golfing buddy, and Joe Hall, an author and friend of my son, Matt. They both provided valuable insight and feedback and helped me believe that this book could have a wider appeal to people who never knew Blase. Additionally, I am very grateful to Hal Smith who not only reviewed the book, but also took the time to write a beautiful foreword.

There are so many others to thank, too numerous to mention here, but they are acknowledged on our website. A special thanks to all of you whose contributions to my first email after Blase's death gave me the inspiration to tell his story by sharing your individual memories of him.

And finally, my sincere thanks to Blase's loving wife, Dawn, and their children, Jason, Brian, and Kevin for your support and mutual commitment to make this happen. I already know this book has helped our family with the healing process. My hope now is that perhaps his story will help inspire others in some way in their journeys through life.

Table of Contents

Foreword

If we have a little bit of luck in this life, each one of us will have the opportunity to meet a truly extraordinary human being that will show us the beauty of God's creation in a transformational way. Blase Cooke was such a person. I had the privilege of knowing Blase for almost thirty years, and during that time, I can honestly say he never ceased to surprise me with the sheer size and diversity of his personality. Every day, Blase got up in the morning and greeted the new day with enthusiasm, filled with the expectation that today was going to be the best day of his life. Here's the real kicker: he was going to share that enthusiasm with everyone he met. In so doing, his spirit had a contagious aspect to it that made all of us who knew him, no matter how peripheral the relationship, feel better about ourselves and the world around us.

Every year, Catholic Charities hosts a golf tournament fund raiser that Blase had chaired from its inception, and every year at the wrap-up dinner, Blase would step to the microphone in front of more than two hundred people to serve as emcee for the evening and announce the prize winners. He was alternately outrageously funny, totally unscripted, and totally focused on touching all the bases that needed to be touched. In this crowd of around two hundred people, Blase probably only knew about half, but every single person in that room felt as though he had known Blase all his life and was sitting at his table, even if it was fifty feet away. He had this unique ability to make the room smaller and bring everybody together. He did it with his family, he did it with his friends, and he did it with complete strangers.

Taking the story of this extraordinary man and giving others the opportunity to experience his magic is not an easy task, but in this book, Phil Cooke, Blase's brother, has done just that. Capturing a spectacular sunrise in words might be a metaphor that would give some idea of the size of the challenge. Phil has a God-given talent for telling stories, and this book has to stand as his finest work. It is a work of love that reflects the man I knew, who still lives on in all our hearts. When you finish this story, I know you, too, will be drawn into that small room and become a friend of Blase Cooke. You will be a richer person for the experience.

Hal Smith
Executive Director,
Catholic Charities of Baltimore

Preface

This is a story about a very normal person who grew up in a very normal family in a typical lower middle-class, blue-collar neighborhood in Baltimore, Maryland. His name is Joseph Peter Cooke, Jr., but from the day he was born on February 3, 1947, all of his family and friends knew him as Blase. He received the name Blase because he was born on the feast of St. Blase. On October 2, 2007, Blase died of cancer at the age of sixty. In this day and age, cancer causes many deaths, and in one way or another, I suspect cancer affects practically every family in America.

So, why write a book about a normal guy like Blase, who lived in a normal family, worked in the construction industry, and died of cancer like so many other people? The truth of the matter is this didn't start out to be a book, but rather, a family memoir that would describe the life of a really good and kind person. The idea was to share this memoir with family and friends. Within hours after he died, when my wife, Wanda, and I were driving back to our home in northern Virginia, I decided I wanted—perhaps I needed—to document as much as I could about his life to help keep his spirit alive for reasons that will become abundantly clear throughout this book. I also thought this would be a catharsis for me to allow me to get through my grieving period by focusing on all the wonderful memories and moments we shared with him over so many years. You see, Blase was not only my big brother, he was my best friend. And as you will read later, Blase had many "best friends."

The next day, October 3, 2007, was the first of a two-day period at the funeral parlor where people would pay their last respects to Blase, his wife, Dawn, and their three sons, Jason, Brian, and Kevin. Before we knew it, the funeral parlor was filled with a huge throng of family, friends, employees, golfing buddies, business associates, and many, many others from all walks of Blase's life. And it remained that way for the next two days. People just wanted to see Blase one last time. For many of them, they had not physically seen him for perhaps two years

11

or more because of his cancer challenges and resulting paralysis. We were amazed at how many people had come to say goodbye. What was even more amazing was it seemed as if every person had his or her own personal story about Blase and how he had impacted his or her life. It was then I realized there was much about Blase we didn't know, and having known him my entire life, I thought I knew him very well.

But there is another, equally important event that occurred which made me realize this family memoir could be more than just memories of Blase shared among family and friends. I arrived at the funeral home early to meet with Jason, Brian, and Kevin to review the drafts of our eulogies we would deliver at his funeral Mass the following day. Blase's youngest son, Kevin, began to review his eulogy with us, and he made the following statement which really hit me: "The story of my father hasn't been written. There is no book out there that you can read to understand the lessons he has taught me. You, however, can be the authors of this unwritten manuscript. I encourage you to continue to tell your stories of my father. There is a lesson to be learned in each and every story you have, and they should be shared." Like all of our family, Kevin, too, heard the many stories being told about Blase. He also knew how fortunate he was to have a dad, a role model in every sense of the word, who showed him how to lead a good life by his example. Now I'm thinking, is God sending me a message? Could a book about my brother's life help someone become a better person, or perhaps help a family through their cancer ordeal or another challenge facing them? Kevin's perceptive comment about his dad, his hero, along with all the wonderful comments we heard from so many people in the days following his death, suggested that perhaps a book about my brother could potentially help a lot of people.

My Brother, My Keeper

Blase was an amazing person who affected an enormous number of people in a very special way. You see, Blase had an amazingly strong, positive attitude and outlook on life, and he lived it, day in and day out. He refused to think in a negative manner. It's what made him so special to so many people he encountered throughout his life, whether it was a family member, a friend, a new employee, a homeless person, or the Governor of Maryland. I feel I am a better person because I knew Blase, and countless others expressed that same sentiment at his funeral service.

So I decided I would solicit the many friends, relatives, coworkers and other acquaintances of Blase to ask them if they would be kind enough to provide their story on how Blase may have impacted their lives. By doing so, perhaps we would come up with sufficient information to warrant a book. In the worst case scenario, I would have captured a more complete picture of my brother's life for our family and friends. In either case, it would be worth the effort.

The fact that you are reading these words tells you that, thanks to a lot of wonderful people, we were able to accomplish our objective of writing this book. What follows is a story about a person whom I think you will like, one from who you may learn, and hopefully, who may inspire you to become a better person. Blase was all about family, faith, hard work, and fun. This book is about how he handled his success in life—with humility and gratitude. More importantly, this book is about how he handled his adversity in life—with courage, conviction, determination, and faith.

Thanks, Blaser.

There are two other items I would like to share. At the end of each chapter, you will see a "Thought for the Day." Blase was not shy about his desire to share what he thought was important in life, much of which centered on having a positive attitude, working hard, and sharing his good fortune with others. He read about and listened to the truly great leaders and motivational speakers of the past and present. At some point, he decided to share some of these great words with his employees, and the sharing expanded to family and friends. I thought it would be appropriate to share some of these thoughts with you. I think you might agree how important a positive thought or story might be during a time in your life when you may need it most. In Blase's case, he had filled his life with a positive attitude, which I am sure helped him through some of his toughest times.

I mentioned earlier that we received some wonderful stories from many of Blase's friends, relatives, and coworkers. I have included many of these stories throughout the book, and I have also included some additional stories in a section at the end of the book entitled, "Memories of Blase."

Finally, if this book can help you, a family member, a friend, or perhaps someone you don't even know through a tough time, then my goal will have been achieved.

Chapter 1

Fundraiser for My Brother's Keeper—
Woodlawn, MD, April 27, 2005
A Salute to Blase Cooke

Because hope needs a home. Motivated by love for God,
My Brother's Keeper seeks to inspire hope and transform the Irvington
community by providing quality services in a respectful, compassionate
and supportive environment.

My Brother's Keeper

On April 27, 2005, more than one thousand people gathered at a gala dinner to honor Joseph Peter Cooke Jr., better known to his family and friends as Blase. The real reason for the dinner was to raise funds to help construct a new building for My Brother's Keeper, a ministry dedicated to helping the less fortunate. A few months prior to this event, Blase was approached by two of his good friends who asked Blase if he would get involved to help raise the money needed to get the building started. In spite of the fact that Blase was approaching his fourth year battling cancer, he agreed to do whatever he could to help. The existing My Brother's Keeper was a small, 900 square-foot soup kitchen that provided a daily meal for people in need. It is located in a community called Irvington in the southwestern section of Baltimore City, and it happened to be the community where Blase was born and grew up. In fact, the original facility was just two doors away from the movie theatre where we spent many Saturday afternoons in our early years. The current neighborhood is not quite the same as it was in our youth, but it was still home in the hearts of many of the families who grew up there in the 1950s. In Blase's case, he never forgot where he came from, and he had a strong affinity to Irvington. The new 4,500 square-foot building would be located just up the street from the existing facility and would offer many more services to help the needy.

What Blase didn't know was that the facility he was going to help build would be called The J. P. Blase Cooke Center and the dinner that evening would be in his honor. The real challenge was not so much related to how many people would attend or if they would be generous. There were so many people who Blase had touched during his life, there was no doubt the event itself would be very successful. No, the real challenge was keeping the secret from Blase. You see, Blase was a real "hands-on" leader. When he got involved in something, he really got involved. Some might say he was a control freak (did I just say that?), but I would never say that. Many things were done to keep the secret: fake invitations, fake speakers, who the honoree would be for the evening, etc. To be perfectly honest, if he knew he was going to be the honoree, he would have probably declined and suggested a more deserving person. That was the kind of guy Blase was.

There was a another reason why Blase didn't discover the secret. In December, 2004, at the time he agreed to lead the fundraising effort for My Brother's Keeper, he was about to undertake a new round of chemotherapy. He had been fighting carcinoid cancer since May, 2001. By this point, he had already undergone major lung and liver surgeries, as well as numerous other invasive procedures, but the cancer continued to spread. This would be his second round of chemotherapy, and this round definitely took a toll on him. Immediately after receiving the treatment, Blase and his wife, Dawn, flew to their home in Florida for most of the winter so he could recuperate in the warmer weather. So a combination of the cancer, the chemo, being in Florida, etc., helped keep the event a secret. Our only concern now was whether he would he be strong enough and physically able to attend the event in his honor.

April 27 was a beautiful spring day in Baltimore. The event was held at Martin's West, one of the finest reception/catering facilities in town. If you have lived in Baltimore for any amount of time, you have probably been to Martin's West. Blase and Dawn returned from Florida in early April and he was feeling much better, although still physically weak. Almost four years of fighting cancer would make anyone weak. But his mind was very sharp. Just a few days before the event, it was decided we needed to tell Blase the event was going to be in his honor. He was starting to suspect something was going on because he was not getting all of the details about the event that he would have normally expected. As far as he knew, he was going to be making a speech about growing up in Irvington and the importance of remembering your roots and giving back to the less fortunate. By this time, it was too late to change anything, so he was told he was going to be the honoree. What he didn't know was the new facility would be named in his honor. He was also unaware there would be a few other surprises.

The entire affair was a most memorable evening. When Blase arrived, he was overwhelmed with well-wishers. There were many family, friends, and business associates who had not seen him for quite a while. Because of his illness, Blase didn't always have the time or energy to take visitors or socialize as much as he would have liked. There were people from all walks of life attending the fundraiser: family, friends, employees, business partners, golfing buddies, priests, and politicians. When Blase arrived, an informal greeting line suddenly appeared and nearly everyone waited in a very long line to get the opportunity to greet him, hug him, and wish him well. His adrenalin must have been pumping hard because he stood there for over an hour embracing and thanking everyone for coming. When Blase finally walked into the room, he was really overwhelmed. If you have ever had the opportunity to attend a seated dinner for more than 1,000 people, you would probably agree it would be a pretty impressive sight. And it was. The staff at Martin's West had done a beautiful job, not only with the room, but the food and service as well. And thanks to Marty Resnick, the owner of Martin's West and a friend of Blase, a share of Martin's profit for that evening went back to My Brother's Keeper in the form of a donation.

The celebration drew many who wanted to give thanks and acknowledge Blase for his generosity and kindness. This may have been the first time in the history of Maryland politics where a former Democratic Governor, William Donald Schaeffer, and the then current Republican Governor, Robert Ehrlich, would be at the same event honoring the same man!

His Eminence, William Cardinal Keeler of Baltimore, was in Rome to help elect Pope Benedict and actually left Rome a day earlier than planned because he did not want to miss the opportunity to honor Blase. Not only were we honored with the very kind words he bestowed upon Blase, but the cardinal also offered his personal reflections regarding the process of electing Pope Benedict XVI. He spoke of the awesome responsibility he and his fellow cardinals felt, as well as how humbled they were to be in that situation. The best news of all, he said, was they were able to elect a pope in time for him to get back to honor Blase.

Ben Civiletti, former Attorney General under the Carter Administration and a longtime golfing buddy of Blase, was the emcee that evening. And finally, Fr. Michael Murphy, the Chairman of the Board of Directors for My Brother's Keeper, and the driving force behind the expansion project, provided a touching overview of how this new building would expand their ability to help so many more disadvantaged people in the Irvington area. Over the next few years, Fr. Mike would also play a crucial role in guiding Blase spiritually through his cancer journey. In addition to the luminaries present, Blase was also honored and/or roasted by myself and two lifelong friends from the Irvington days, Charlie Rose and David Carney.

Blase poses for a photo with the two governors and Cardinal Keeler. *Photo courtesy of MattSpanglerPhoto.com*

Although the event was to celebrate Blase, more importantly, it was all about raising awareness of the expanded ministry of My Brother's Keeper. That one evening alone raised over $550,000. As a result of that initial fundraising event, the groundbreaking took place on September 17, 2005, and the construction of the new building was completed and formally dedicated on May 21, 2006. Unfortunately, due to his illness, Blase was unable to attend either event in person. This fundraiser has become an annual event, and in 2006, former Governor William Donald Schaeffer was the proud recipient of the first J.P. Blase Cooke Award. In 2007, David Carney, a longtime close friend of Blase and prominent lawyer in Howard County, Maryland, became the second recipient. And the most recent event in 2008 honored Mr. Bill Franey, who first met Blase through business and then became very close friends. All of these gentlemen were honored for their contributions to helping the poor and needy throughout the greater Baltimore community. These three events raised an additional $800,000 for My Brother's Keeper. The plan is to continue raising money for this very worthy cause.

Since the opening of the new building, My Brother's Keeper has been able to expand its services. They are now providing a daily meal to an even larger number of clients. In addition, they are offering Alcoholics and Narcotics Anonymous meetings, parenting classes, job-readiness programs, and after-school programs. The new facility now stands as a symbol of hope and renewal for the entire Irvington area.

It's very rare to find one person who has the ability to reach out and make a profound impact on so many people from so many different walks of life. Blase's life was consumed with serving and helping others, and his love of family and God was so apparent to many. Somehow, he was able to make this connection with people in a positive and impactful way.

I mentioned earlier there would be a few other surprises for Blase. From a speaker's perspective, we were asked to "roast" Blase on this special evening by recalling one of Blase's all-time favorite stories. Below is my "salute."

Phil's Salute to Blase

So many stories and so little time. When I was asked to tell my favorite story about "The Donald," I mean, "The Blaser," I struggled because I have known him all my life and there have been so many great stories. Dave Carney, our Committee Chairman, stipulated that I was only permitted to tell you one story—so, unfortunately, I will not be able mention the time when Blase was nine years old, and he got a bow and arrow set for his birthday and proceeded to remove the rubber tips, sharpen the arrow head, and shoot our sister, Jul, in the leg, and it stuck!

I also won't be to tell the story when Blase was arrested for drag racing, or the time he totaled our 1960 Chevy in the heart of Irvington when he was home on leave from the army. I wish I had time to tell you about the fist fight Blase had at Benny's

Pool Hall with a rather large and muscular off-duty cop, who years later became our brother-in-law. He married the sister with the hole in her leg. Speaking of fist fights, please raise your hand if you were ever involved in a brawl on a family vacation at Disney World. Blase was.

So after a lot of thought, I decided to share with everyone here this evening one of both mine and Blase's favorite stories about Blase entitled, "How I hurt my back in Las Vegas." As many of you know, Blase has had chronic back problems for many years. In fact, for all of us who have competed in various sports and games with Blase, you would typically hear Blase complain about his back problems on those rare occasions when he lost a bet. But back to the Vegas story. It happened about twenty years ago. Blase was the president of the Associated Builders and Contractors, and he and Dawn were attending the annual convention in Las Vegas. They arrived in Vegas with their wonderful friends, Jim and Mary Jane Hampson, the day before Blase was to address the 1,500 or so folks attending the boondoggle, I mean, convention.

Dawn and Blase had agreed to meet Mary Jane and Jim in the lobby of the hotel. They were going to have a drink prior to going to dinner at the most expensive restaurant Dawn could find. Due to flight schedules, time changes, and various other challenges that face us when we travel, Blase had not really had the opportunity to "take care of business," if you know what I mean. In other words, when everyone met in the lobby, Blase had a desperate need to find a restroom. At this point you might be saying to yourselves, "What does this have to do with a bad back?" Bear with me.

As Blase began to walk away to find the rest room he turned and promised everyone, "I'll be back in few minutes," whereupon Dawn said, "You better be because we have a reservation and

I don't want to be late." Earlier that day, Blase went down to the convention area of the hotel to check everything out, and he remembered seeing a restroom there. Since there was no activity in the convention area that evening, he also realized it would be quiet and private. He walked into one of the largest restrooms he had ever seen and quickly realized he had the whole place to himself. I remember him telling me there must have been forty stalls in there. After carefully selecting his stall he began to settle in – and then it happened. KAPOW!! HIS BACK GOES OUT!!

Now we really have a problem. Blase can't get off the toilet seat, he's in terrible pain, there is no one around to help him, and perhaps his biggest dilemma of all is that he only has few minutes before he screws up Dawn's dinner reservation. He knew he had to act immediately, so Blase gathered up all the strength he could muster, and somehow, was able to extricate himself from the toilet seat. Although still in serious pain, Blase, the man with that incredibly positive attitude, felt good that he was making progress—until he realized that his pants and underwear were still around his ankles.

All of the sudden, he heard a noise toward the front of the restroom. Someone had come in. He opened the door of his stall, and still in pain, managed to shuffle out of the stall into the open space. Now I want you to visualize what we have here: two strangers, inexplicably brought together by fate, one just minding his own business, and the other about to make a very strange request.

As soon as the person came into his view, Blase called out, "Sir, excuse me, sir, but I really need your help. My back went out and I am in terrible pain. Could you please help me?" The man was about forty feet from Blase and about four feet from the door to freedom when he suddenly notices that Blase is half-naked. So let me ask you, what would you do if you were in this situation? Somehow Blase convinces this guy to walk toward him. Now he has to convince him to pull up his pants and help him out of the bathroom.

Now let's try to put this in perspective. We all know Blase has achieved some major accomplishments throughout his life. But I would submit to you that getting a complete stranger to pull up a another stranger's pants in an empty bathroom in the middle of Sin City has got to rank as one of Blase's all-time major achievements. Needless to say, Blase did make it to dinner that night, and Blase, I am so happy that all of us are here tonight to share this dinner with you.

On behalf of your family and friends, thanks for being such a great role model, leader, husband, father, grandfather, and brother, and an inspiration to us all.

Blase and Dawn with their boys and their spouses.
Photo courtesy of MattSpanglerPhoto.com

Phil Cooke

As mentioned earlier, Fr. Mike Murphy is one of the driving forces behind the ongoing success of My Bother's Keeper. Fr. Mike is a wonderful human being and a very giving and generous person. The salute to Blase that evening was, for the most part, a "roast" of Blase, as evidenced by my story above. But the real salute came from Fr. Mike at Blase's passing when he expressed the following:

Blase's commitment to the less fortunate was generous, with his leadership guiding many charitable organizations. His hand steered commissions, directed panels, and piloted elected officials and advocacy groups toward strong partnerships. He was also a devoted husband, father, and parishioner, having served on the board of his archdiocese. In every endeavor, his character, common sense, sound judgment, and willingness to strive made him an exemplary friend, citizen, and inspiration.

Truly, Blase was his brother's keeper.

Memorandum

To: All Personnel

From: Blase Cooke

Re: THOUGHT FOR THE DAY

"Dear God,
So far today,
I've done alright.
I haven't gossiped.
I haven't lost my temper,
I haven't lied or cheated,
I haven't been greedy, grumpy,
Nasty, selfish, or over-indulgent.
I am very thankful for that.
But in a few minutes, Lord,
I'm going to get out of bed,
And from then on, I'm probably
Going to need a lot more help.
Amen."

Chapter 2

Joseph Peter Cooke Jr.—February 3, 1947
Blase Arrives

"Somehow he just figured it out on his own . . ."

On February 3, 1947, the first of five children was born to Joseph and Phyllis Cooke. He was named Joseph Peter Cooke Jr., after his father. What a strong name! These were two of the greatest saints in the history of the Catholic church. Blase was born on the Feast Day of St. Blase, and from day one, he was immediately called Blase, I guess so there wouldn't be any confusion between he and dad having the same name. And the name stuck.

There is not a lot that is known about St. Blase. It is believed he was born and lived primarily in the latter part of the third century, and he came from a wealthy Christian family. In the early years of his life, St. Blase focused on the study of philosophy and later became a physician because he wanted to help people. After witnessing so much physical misery as a physician, he decided to become a priest and spend the rest of his days in the service of God by helping people both physically, and more importantly, spiritually. He later became a bishop in the town of Sebaste in Armenia, which is now modern-day Turkey. St. Blase worked hard to help his people become holy and happy.

When the governor of Cappadocia began to persecute Christians, St. Blase was one of those captured and sent to prison to be beheaded. On the way, people crowded the road to see their beloved bishop for the last time. He blessed them all, including the pagans. A poor mother rushed up to him. She begged him to save her child who was choking to death from a fishbone. The saint whispered a prayer and blessed the child. He worked a miracle that saved the child's life. That is why St. Blase is called upon by all who have throat diseases. On his feast day, we have our throats blessed. We ask him to protect us from all sicknesses of the throat. While in prison, St. Blase converted many pagans. Despite constant torture, he never gave up his faith in Jesus. He was believed to have been beheaded in the year 316 A.D.

I find it pleasantly ironic that Blase would grow up with traits very similar to St. Blase—hard-working, extremely faithful, enduring tremendous physical pain, and focused on helping people. I also find it ironic that Blase's cancer spread to his throat. Fortunately, the procedures he had to remove those tumors were successful. Perhaps St. Blase was looking out for his namesake.

***

Our mom grew up on 1816 South Light Street, about a ten-minute walk from Baltimore's now famous Inner Harbor. Back then, the Inner Harbor was a somewhat seedy area of warehouses and homeless people. Dad was born and raised in the southwestern part of Baltimore City, just off Washington Boulevard. The area was, and still is, affectionately known as Pigtown. The name originates from the 1800s when the Baltimore and Ohio Railroad released its cargo of pigs to run through the city's streets to the slaughterhouses in South Baltimore. They both came from large, lower middle-class families. Joe and Phyllis met just months before Pearl Harbor. And like so many others of that "Greatest Generation," World War II brought all other plans and dreams to a screeching halt. Joe enlisted in the army, and during the war, spent most of his time in Africa and India, while Phyllis and her twin sister, Rita, worked in a factory just down the street from where they lived. The factory was converted into manufacturing parachutes and other materials to assist in the war effort. Shortly after he returned from overseas, Joe and Phyllis were married on April 22, 1946. They moved into a tiny two-bedroom rowhome in the southwest part of Baltimore City in a little hamlet called Irvington.

There were three prominent features about this small, blue-collar town. First, the town is literally surrounded by dead people. There were three large cemeteries that bordered Irvington—Loudon Park Cemetery, New Cathedral Cemetery, and the Baltimore National Cemetery. Our house on 21 S. Monastery Avenue was just across the street from the New Cathedral Cemetery. You could actually see the gravestones from our front porch. In fact, our early years of growing up were spent horsing around both inside and outside of the cemetery. There was a small empty lot just down the street where we played baseball and football, and we used to scale the fence and play inside the cemetery because there was a stream which flowed into a sewer system. The sewer "tunnel" was one of our most adventurous activities we undertook as kids because you could walk into the tunnel on Monastery Avenue and end up approximately three blocks away on Hilton Street. I don't ever remember walking through that tunnel without my big brother, Blase, leading the way.

Another major characteristic of this community is St. Joseph Monastery Church, one of the largest and most beautiful churches in all of Baltimore. We grew up walking to the church and to the St. Joseph Monastery Grade School, just down the street from the church. It was, and still is, one of the major anchor points of Irvington. The Church of the Most Holy Passion, the "old church," as we knew it, was consecrated in 1867. The "new" monastery church was consecrated in 1932. Since the inception of the church, it has been ministered by the Passionist Order. Today, the church focuses on ministries that include helping those in need of finding their faith and the poor and underprivileged in the area.

The third significant landmark of Irvington is Mt. St. Joseph High School, which was dedicated on Thanksgiving Day, 1876. I will talk more about Mt. St. Joe later, as it played a very important role in Blase's life. He was a very proud honorary graduate of Mt. St. Joe's class of 2003, even though he only attended the school for one year back in 1961.

Shortly after Phyllis and Joe settled into their tiny home in Irvington, they immediately got to work on having a family. If you do the math, you will realize that Blase was born approximately nine and one-half months after the Joe and Phyllis were married. Virtually everyone in that generation had lots of catching up to do, and apparently they were not fooling around, or perhaps they were. In any case, Blase was soon to have a number of siblings sharing that two-bedroom home on Monastery Avenue.

Mary Agnes (Aggie) was born fifteen months later on May 6, 1948. I was born nineteen months after Aggie on December 3, 1949, and our sister, Julia Anne, was born on May 7, 1951. Finally, little brother Greg was born on November 8, 1956. So, to summarize this math project, our parents produced five kids in just over a ten-year period. I suspect these kinds of numbers were fairly common for a post-WWII Catholic family.

Needless to say, that home on Monastery Avenue was bursting at the seams. Before we finally moved into a larger home in the summer of 1959, Blase and I had spent a few years sleeping on a "Hollywood bed" in the front bedroom with Mom and Dad. Believe me when I tell you there was nothing "Hollywood" about that bed or those sleeping arrangements. Aggie and Jul slept together in the back bedroom and shared their room with Greg after he was born. It now occurs to me why it may have taken Mom and Dad so long before Greg finally arrived on the scene!

There were many friends and relatives who lived in the neighborhood who we spent time with as well. Two of Dad's five sisters lived in the neighborhood. Aunt Madge, Uncle Vernon, and our cousin, Adele, lived just up the street, and Aunt Jul and our cousin, Eileen, lived almost directly across the alley. Aunt Jul's husband, Uncle Eddie, was killed in an auto accident in 1948 when Eileen was only six months old. We never knew him. My mom's twin sister, Rita, and Uncle Bill Walsh lived about a block away. They had seven children: Michael, Dennis, Eileen, Kathleen, Patrick, Helen, and Mary Monica. Unfortunately, they lost little Helen to pneumonia when she was ten months old. We didn't really hear or talk much about Helen's passing until we were older.

Perhaps the most significant event I can remember from those days growing up on Monastery Avenue was when Uncle Bill died on February 5, 1958, at the young age of forty-one. Aunt Rita met and fell in love with Uncle Bill, and they were married about a year or so before Mom and Dad. Uncle Bill had apparently contracted rheumatic fever during the War, which weakened his heart and he eventually passed away as a result of heart failure.

The day before Uncle Bill died, Blase had just turned eleven years old. In less than two years, he would experience the sudden death of his own father. Since we didn't see Uncle Bill very often, I suspect it didn't have a major impact on Blase. We never actually talked about it, and to my knowledge, Blase never talked with any of Uncle Bill's children about his passing away. Death is hard to talk about, especially at a young age.

There were many happy times and memories growing up on Monastery Avenue. We played all kinds of outdoor games: baseball, football, cowboys and Indians, red line, Simon says, hide and seek. We roller-skated and rode bikes. We took Sunday drives for ice cream cones. And there were those hot summer evenings where it seemed like the entire neighborhood would be out catching lightning bugs and storing them in glass jars, only to find them all expired the next morning.

Phil Cooke

Blase at his First Holy Communion celebration, 1955

Some of the most vivid and fun memories growing up in the fifties were the Saturday afternoon double feature movies playing at the Irvington Theater. There were always chores on Saturday mornings, which often resulted in being rewarded with twenty-five cents, which would get you admission to the double feature movie for fifteen cents and ten pieces of penny candy. What a treat!

Blase's early childhood was typical of most kids growing up in the 1950s. He had lots of childhood friends, and he was always outside playing—I guess because the houses in the neighborhood were so small and the fact that there were no televisions or X-Boxes back then to keep you occupied. Your imagination became your GameBoy.

Perhaps because the houses were so small, we all contracted measles and chicken pox at the same time, although Mom told us later in life that as soon as one of us came down with a contagious illness, she threw all of us into the same room so we would all enjoy the experience at the same time. I think they did it for efficiency's sake and to cut down on the cost of house calls from the doctor. Yes, in the fifties, doctors made house calls.

Blase was an altar boy, which was considered a privilege, or that's what we were told. Our dad was heavily involved in church activities. He was an active member of the Knights of Columbus and also an usher at Mass every Sunday. We always felt very proud watching our dad usher at Mass. He would always dress up in a suit and tie. He handled that collection basket as well as any usher I have ever seen. Being an altar boy did have its privileges. When we served Mass during the week, we had a built-in excuse for coming late to school, and, of course, the Sisters of Notre Dame, who taught us, immediately adopted us as teacher's pets until such time as we might prove otherwise. Serving Mass at a funeral was a choice assignment because you got out of school in the middle of the day. As a young boy, I'm sure Blase had no idea what an impact being an altar boy would have on him later in life. Daily Mass was an integral part of Blase's adult life. I guess old habits die hard.

In addition to all the church and school activities at St. Joseph Monastery, we also enjoyed week-long summer camps at Camp Gabriel located about a one-hour drive away. Camp Gabriel was owned by the church and operated by the Xaverian Brothers and Sisters of Notre Dame. The property included a lake, a large bunkhouse for the kids, a dining hall, picnic grounds, ball fields, and a playground. Blase, Aggie, Jul, and I would each spend a week there during the summer. The weeks would alternate between boys and girls as well as age groups. There were lots of sports, including swimming, hiking, baseball, soccer, and boxing, as well as activities like fishing, checkers, and dominoes. It was a very active, enjoyable, and fun week, and I'm sure it gave mom and dad a brief but well-deserved break, albeit a very short one.

***

Blase was a bit of a prankster growing up, which occasionally would get him in trouble. As the oldest in a family of five siblings, he had opportunities to have fun at his younger siblings' expense. My funniest memory of Blase was actually a prank he pulled on me. I was six or seven years old. We were goofing off outside of our house late one autumn afternoon when he suggested we play cowboys and Indians. He, of course, was the cowboy and he captured me, the Indian. He found some rope and tied me to a lamppost. Then he left. He went back into the house. He apparently never told Mom because when it was time for dinner, she came out to call for me and saw me tied to the lamppost. When Mom saw me, all she could do was laugh. I was initially upset because I fell for the trick. As it turned out, we all ended up having a good laugh over the incident.

***

In August of 1959, we left Irvington and moved to what seemed at the time to be very far away to a home located at 1932 Old Frederick Road in Catonsville, Maryland. It turns out to be just 5.1 miles from the old home in Irvington (I know this now, thanks to Google). One of Dad's other sisters, Aunt Mary, and her husband, Uncle Joe, had moved into a home and Aunt Jul and Eileen moved in with them. Then Madge and Vernon bought a home near them, and before long, we moved into the area as well.

Compared to our previous home, it was a very large house—four bedrooms! It was an old, single-family, two-story clapboard home with a large front porch that was probably built in the 1930s. I'm guessing it was a quarter-acre lot. There were a few fruit trees, old chicken coops, and a detached garage. Unlike the city, there was considerable space to roam and no cemeteries anywhere to be seen, but there was really only one thing that stands out about that house.

On Sunday morning, November 22, 1959, just a few months after we moved in, our dad, Joseph Peter Cooke Sr., died of a massive heart attack at the age of forty-three. He was getting ready to go to the 12:15 p.m. mass at St. Joseph Monastery, where he continued to volunteer as an usher. He was standing in the doorway between the kitchen and dining room drinking a cup of tea. All of the kids were in the living room. I don't remember what we were doing. We heard a loud noise, which was Dad collapsing on the floor, and then we heard Mom screaming. We ran into the next room where we saw dad shaking violently. He was making a sound that none of us will ever forget—guttural sounds, his final breaths.

Mom screamed for one of us to go to the neighbor's house for help, and Jul ran out to the neighbor next door, who was a nurse. Within what seemed to be just a few minutes, there was bedlam in the house. The neighbors were there. The firemen arrived. Aggie had the wherewithal to call our dad's sister, Aunt Julia, who lived around the corner. Then we heard the fireman tell Mom that Dad was dead and there was nothing they could do to bring him back. Mom became hysterical. She fainted. Someone noticed we were all in the room watching and listening to everything, so we were escorted upstairs into a bedroom and they shut the door. We were alone. Then Blase started to cry. Then the rest of us started to cry. At that point, except for maybe Blase, none of us really understood what had just happened, and we especially didn't understand the permanency of it all.

It snowed on the day Dad was buried, and we were told it was a message from the angels in Heaven that Dad had arrived. Christmas was approaching, and somehow Blase got an idea to sell Christmas trees. There were some spruce trees in the back of our house, and Blase decided to cut them down, drag them out to the front of our house, and sell them. I don't remember how many he sold, not that it

35

matters. What I do believe is that we saw a precursor to his work ethic and perhaps an inherent understanding to help support his family.

We never really got to know Dad very well because we didn't see him much when he was alive. Simply put, he worked a lot. After he got back from overseas in 1946, he re-enlisted in the army until November, 1950. After leaving the army, he had a number of jobs. He would put in a full day's work on the day job, then handle bartending duties at night and on weekends. He tended bar at the Old Southern Hotel in downtown Baltimore and also Gannon's Restaurant in Southwest Baltimore. When we were very young, Mom used to take us to eat lunch and visit Dad when he was working at the Southern Hotel. When Dad had to work late, he would sometimes call Mom to ask if we had been good children, and then he would call the local drugstore to have ice cream sundaes delivered—his way of showing his love for his wife and children.

He delivered groceries, worked for the Jewel Tea Company as a route salesman, and sold cookware with his brother, George, who a few years later also died of a heart attack at the age of forty-four. I know our dad, along with his two brothers and brother-in-law, tried a number of business ventures, but we didn't know much about them except for the cookware business. They sold Luster Craft Cookware, and they did it in a very creative way by preparing dinner parties for the host and hostess and their friends (similar to a Tupperware party, except the guests were treated to a sit-down dinner prepared in the cookware). We got involved by helping Dad prep for the dinner by peeling the potatoes and carrots and helping to load up the car for the dinner party that evening.

What we also realized, and appreciated much later in life, was that our dad worked hard and sacrificed to give his wife and children a better life, something that Blase inherently grasped quickly and put into action at a very young age.

As anyone could imagine, the sudden departure of this good man devastated our mom. I'm sure she wanted to get out of that house as quickly as possible. She needed to get back to more familiar surroundings, and especially closer to her twin sister, Rita, who had been coping with being a widow for the past two years. It was the middle of the school year, and four of us were attending St. Agnes Grade School. Poor Greg had turned three years old just two weeks before Dad died. It's very sad to think that he would never get the opportunity to be able to have any personal remembrances of his dad.

It's truly remarkable how lives can change dramatically in an instant. One day, you are smiling and playing with your father, and the next day, he is gone—forever. His life on Earth is over, but your life goes on. Looking back, without really being able to truly comprehend what was happening, our lives as children were about to change in ways we would not realize until we were all much older. In retrospect, what we as kids were going through paled in comparison to what Mom was experiencing. Because we were so young, we didn't understand the incredible trauma Mom was going through. She had just lost her best friend, lover, and partner for life—gone forever.

***

Shortly after the school year finished, we moved back to the Irvington area and the St. Joseph Monastery parish—back home to more familiar surroundings. We moved into a small three-bedroom rowhome in a development called Uplands. Our home on Monastery Avenue was just a block south of the church, whereas our home in Uplands was approximately three blocks west of the church.

Uplands is a small enclave of approximately 150 rowhomes that were built between 1948 and 1950. Our house at 4404 Manorview Road was just slightly larger than the house on Monastery Avenue. Mom, Jul, and Greg shared the larger bedroom in the front of the house. Blase and I shared a bedroom in the back of the house, and somehow, Aggie had her own bedroom. Admittedly, it was very small, but we still never figured out how she pulled that one off. There were two neat features in this house that we did not have in the house on Monastery Avenue: a club basement with a bar, and a back porch.

We were now back "home," back with our old friends and classmates at St. Joseph Monastery Grade School, back to more familiar surroundings, and closer to our Walsh cousins, who now lived about a fifteen-minute walk away. Over the years, there was one constant in the lives of the Cooke and Walsh siblings; a day never passed where Rita and Phyllis didn't have at least one conversation. These two sisters were inseparable. Losing their husbands only made their bond stronger. As families, we were more like brothers and sisters than cousins. Given our Irish heritage and the fact that our moms were identical twins, we obviously looked alike, and over the years, we were often mistaken for being either a Walsh or a Cooke, or a Cooke or a Walsh—you get the picture.

The Cooke and Walsh cousins: (Top Row, L-R) Greg, Pat, Phil, Dennis, Blase, Michael; (Bottom Row) Mary Monica, Jul, Kathleen, Eileen, Mary Agnes

Even to this day, I can't imagine how Mom and Aunt Rita were able to find the strength to handle the loss of their husbands and, at the same time, handle all the responsibilities of raising a large family. In the case of Mom, she was the classic housewife, and Dad was the breadwinner. She was the nurturer, and Dad was the disciplinarian, and when it came to discipline, he was strict, but always fair. You did not ever want to hear Mom say, "Wait until your father gets home."

Suddenly, Mom was thrust into a daunting situation. She no longer had someone to handle some very crucial responsibilities. She did the best she could, but it was very difficult. To put it bluntly, she was overwhelmed, she was lost, and she was hurting. Mom's life had changed forever. She was a supportive and loving wife and mother, who relied on her husband for many things, and in an instant, it was all gone.

Soon after we moved, the nightmares started. Perhaps they had started right after Dad died, we don't really know. The house on Old Frederick Road was probably large enough to mute her screams, but after we moved into the smaller home in Uplands, we very often heard Mom crying out Dad's name and wailing. She had those dreams for years. She never talked about the dreams, and we didn't push her to tell us. All we knew was she was in pain. I always thought that her nightmare was reliving that day, again and again. There was a huge hole in her heart, which never really healed.

Almost twenty-five years later, we were to learn that Mom was clinically depressed and dependent on prescription drugs—librium and valium. She started taking those drugs not long after Dad died. The psychologist told us that she had never gotten over Dad's death. Don't get me wrong, we had a wonderful and loving mom. She was funny, she did her best to keep her children on the straight and narrow, and she was always there for us.

***

After dad's death, Blase had to grow up very fast, and he did. He returned to his final year of grammar school at St. Joseph Monastery. Mom was now totally responsible for raising her young family on monthly checks from Social Security and veterans' benefits. By default, Blase had suddenly and perhaps subconsciously taken on new responsibilities. At the age of thirteen, he could not have fully understood the financial pressures facing Mom, but he must have sensed something, because he quickly found his first job delivering newspapers. After graduating from grade school, he took on a second job working at a sub shop. He was looking forward to moving on to high school and had been accepted to Mt. St. Joseph High School.

Most kids we knew who attended private Catholic grade schools typically would continue on to private Catholic high schools. This was certainly the case in Baltimore in the early sixties. For the most part, the Baltimore City School System was not known for its academic excellence, and to be candid, segregation among Blacks and Whites was still very prevalent. The African-American community was largely centered in the inner city, but in the early sixties had started to integrate into predominantly White neighborhoods located near the outskirts of the city. Irvington was one of the many areas where the racial makeup was changing rapidly. For many reasons, Baltimore City, like many other major metropolitan areas around the country, had serious racial issues throughout the decade of the sixties. For example, there was a local TV dance show that aired daily called *The Buddy Dean Show*, which was very similar to the more famous Dick Clark's *American Bandstand*. There were dancers who auditioned and won spots as regular "Committee Members" on the show. Then there were other teens who would apply and be selected to attend as guests for one of the daily shows. Except for one day a month called "Negro Day," the dancers were all White. Perhaps you might be familiar with the original movie *Hairspray*, the Tony Award-winning Broadway play of the same name, or the remake of the movie

with John Travolta, which was based on the original, Baltimore-based
Buddy Dean Show.

The Baltimore City Public School System was similar in that the city
schools were becoming more and more predominantly Black as more
and more Whites were moving out of the city to Baltimore and Anne
Arundel County. If you were White and living in the city, you either
went to a city school or you chose to attend a private school. Of
course, you had to be able to afford the expense of a private school.

Because Mom was a widow, most, if not all of the tuition for Catholic
grade school was waived. But that wasn't the case for a private
Catholic high school like Mt. St. Joe. Mom was new at handling the
family finances, so she probably didn't even think about the potential
impact of an annual tuition commitment of $300.00, plus books and
other expenses. At that time, she was only receiving about $350.00 per
month to support her entire family.

Blase apparently did understand the impact, because at the end of his
first year at Mt. St. Joe, he told Mom he did not want to go back. He
also realized that Aggie had just graduated from grade school, and
Mom naturally wanted all her children to attend a Catholic high
school. He knew Mom would not be able to afford both tuitions. Aggie
ended up attending St. Martin's High School, which, of all the
Catholic girls private schools in Baltimore, was much less expensive
than the others. Blase continued to work part-time jobs and, at the age
of fourteen, he removed the only financial burden that he could control
by opting out of Mt. St. Joe. In his case, instead of walking one block
down the street to Mt. St. Joe, a private boys' school, Blase would now
walk one block up the street to Edmonson High School, a public coed school where he would finish out his high school career. The
following year, when I was ready for high school, I was very fortunate
to receive a full grant to Mt. St. Joe. My old baseball and basketball
coach from St. Joseph Monastery, Mr. John Vicchio, "Mr. Vic," knew

of our family situation and recommended me to some very generous friends who were kind enough to foot the bill, enabling me to attend Mt. St. Joe. By the time Jul was ready for high school, and the older kids were all working, Mom was able to afford her tuition at Archbishop Keough High School, which had just opened its doors. I should point out that we all followed Blase's example of working part-time jobs. Aggie and Jul worked as babysitters and student nurses or "Pinkies" at Bon Secours Hospital, while I had jobs delivering newspapers, working at the local drugstore, and the U.S. Postal Service. Years later, Greg also attended Mt. St. Joe and graduated in 1974. And yes, he worked part-time jobs as well. Unknowingly, Blase seemed to have inherited our father's work ethic, and he became a role model for his younger siblings.

Although Blase only attended Mt. St. Joe for one year, the school had a profound impact on him. I think this experience helped him to learn very early on that life is not always fair. He also learned he had to accept this situation and not let it get the best of him. Forty-one years later, in 2003, he finally received his diploma from Mt. St. Joseph High School. He was awarded an honorary diploma. Blase was not able to attend his four-year term at the "Mount," but his three sons were privileged to do so. Blase also helped a number of other worthy students attend the Mount by establishing a trust fund to assist young men living in west Baltimore who did not have the financial resources to attend.

It was also evident that Blase had a profound impact on Mt. St. Joe. Below is an excerpt from a beautiful tribute to Blase from Barry Fitzpatrick, the Principal at Mt. St. Joe.

Dear Parents, Students, and Friends of the Mount,

For the past several years, each morning as we would announce our prayer intentions for the day, we would say the name of Blase Cooke, honorary graduate of 2003, and every now and then, there would be a student who would ask who this man was. Last month, as I took eleven of our students to Mr. Cooke's funeral at Saint Louis Church in Clarksville, one of our seniors said to me as we were leaving, "He must have been one incredible man." Indeed he was, and I would like to do my best to tell all of you who he was, knowing full well I could not do justice to him in this short space.

I first met Blase and his wife, Dawn, in the late 1980s as their oldest son, Jason, was a student here. Jason graduated in 1990, followed by his brothers, Brian '94, and Kevin '95. Blase could be found with Dawn cheering Jason on at lacrosse games, at any number of our parent meetings, or just passing through his old neighborhood here in Irvington. His positive attitude about life permeated every interaction he ever had with people, as did his Catholic faith.

In 2003, I needed a way to convince Blase to come to our graduation without his knowing that we were going to bestow an honorary diploma on him. Blase was the head of Harkins Builders, having worked his way up from laborer after his discharge from the U.S. Army to become president. His mentor and founder of the company, Tom Harkins, and Tom's wife, Dottie, sent their son, Tommie, to Our Lady of Good Counsel early in my teaching career. Dottie had a grandson, Paul Santucci, graduating in 2003, so I enlisted her aid in getting Blase to the ceremony under the guise of honoring her. It worked. Dawn, his two brothers, and two of his sons, and Dottie all helped conspire to surprise Blase, which, he assured me later, was no easy task. One of my favorite pictures of him is from that day with him smiling broadly and holding his Mount Saint Joseph diploma. Believe me, it was a small token indeed to say thank you to a man who gave us his two brothers, his sons, and so much more by the support he showed us all his life long.

About seven years ago, Blase was diagnosed with cancer, and he fought it with the valiant nature that was his alone. Our own Father Mike ministered to him for much of that time, and Blase was deeply moved to see the renovated My Brother's Keeper in Irvington named after him. With Father Mike's help and initiative, Blase had backed that project with all his might as a testament to the neighborhood in which he and his family had grown up and for which Blase had the fondest of memories. Again, his faith and his commitment to give back took over as he convinced so many to see this project to its completion. Giving back was part of this man's DNA.

It was never in his nature to seek recognition for himself. He had humility down pat, and he strove with every fiber of his being to impart that virtue to all with whom he came into contact. The Xaverian Brothers Fundamental Principles says:

> *Affirm your brothers and sisters in their gifts,*
> *for by doing so you enable them*
> *to realize the gifts that God has given them*
> *for His service.*
> *In turn,*
> *allow them to affirm you*
> *and call you forth for even greater service*
> *of the Lord.*

My Brother, My Keeper

Blase Cooke is as good a man as I have ever known. He understood the strength that comes from being gentle with others, and he used all of his talents for the benefit of those around him. He was a builder by profession, and, I think, by vocation as well. He built relationships, fed them, kept them alive, realizing all the while that God's work here on Earth must truly be our own. May he rest in peace.

Sincerely,

Barry J. Fitzpatrick
Principal

Blase receiving his diploma in May, 2003 with Brian, Dawn, and Kevin

Memorandum

To: All Personnel

From: Blase Cooke

Re: THOUGHT FOR THE DAY

You may have seen this already. It is one of my favorites. Enjoy.

MAYONNAISE JAR and 2 CUPS OF COFFEE

When things in your life seem almost too much to handle, when twenty-four hours in a day is not enough, remember the mayonnaise jar and two cups of coffee.

A professor stood before his philosophy class and had some items in front of him. When the class began, wordlessly, he picked up a very large and empty mayonnaise jar and proceeded to fill it with golf balls.

He then asked the students if the jar was full. They agreed that it was.

The professor then picked up a box of pebbles and poured them into the jar. He shook the jar lightly. The pebbles rolled into the open areas between the golf balls.

He then asked the students again if the jar was full. They agreed it was.

The professor next picked up a box of sand and poured it into the jar. Of course, the sand filled up everything else.

My Brother, My Keeper

He asked once more if the jar was full.

The students responded with an unanimous "yes."

The professor then produced two cups of coffee from under the table and poured the entire contents into the jar, effectively filling the empty space between the sand. The students laughed.

"Now," said the professor, as the laughter subsided, "I want you to recognize that this jar represents your life. The golf balls are the important things—relationship with the Lord, family, children, health, friends, and favorite passions—things that if everything else was lost and only they remained, your life would still be full.

The pebbles are the other things that matter like your job, house, and car.

The sand is everything else— the small stuff.

"If you put the sand into the jar first," he continued, "there is no room for the pebbles or the golf balls. The same goes for life."

"If you spend all your time and energy on the small stuff, you will never have room for the things that are important to you."

"So . . .
Pay attention to the things that are critical to your happiness.
Play with your children. Take time to get medical checkups.
Take your partner out to dinner."

Phil Cooke

"Play another eighteen. There will always be time to clean the house and fix the disposal."

"Take care of the golf balls first—the things that really matter. Set your priorities. The rest is just sand."

One of the students raised her hand and inquired what the coffee represented. The professor smiled. "I'm glad you asked. It just goes to show you that no matter how full your life may seem, there's always room for a couple cups of coffee with a friend."

Chapter 3

The Wedding—September 22, 1968

"I was attracted to the guy in the blue button-down shirt, khaki pants, loafers, and a frat jacket . . ."

Dawn Klinger, December 9, 1966

The day before Blase and Dawn's wedding, the Cooke family made the four-hour trek north on I-95 from Baltimore, Maryland to Paterson, New Jersey. The trip was uneventful, that is, until we arrived. We met Blase and Dawn at her parents' house and then proceeded to follow them to Aunt Carol's home, where we would be staying for the weekend. Blase and Dawn were sitting at a red light in their brand-new baby blue 1968 Volkswagen when suddenly, a car came whizzing around the corner and crashed into the left front of their car. It was a mess, and it was less than a day before Blase and Dawn were to begin their new life, happily ever after. The police were called, and it was determined the driver was under age and had no insurance. The car was towed to the shop for repairs. Blase and Dawn had to hitch a ride with other family members in order to make it to the church for the rehearsal that evening.

Since Dawn's parents, Bill and Jean Klinger, never had a formal wedding, and since this was their first daughter to be married, they pulled out all the stops. There were 120 family and friends who attended, and practically all of them were from Dawn's side of the family. The honeymoon was short. It was a "one-night stand" in a little motel just off the New Jersey turnpike. They were fortunate in that they checked into a room with a coin-operated vibrating bed and Blase just happened to have a pocketful of quarters. To their chagrin, the damn thing didn't work. So the next day, with the honeymoon behind them, they jumped in a borrowed car and headed south on I-95 to start their new life together. Dawn cried during most of the trip to Baltimore because she realized that, except for one or two weekend visits a year, she was more than likely leaving home for good. They moved into a small two-bedroom apartment for $115 per month. Our sister, Aggie, and her husband lived in an apartment just across the street, and Mom was only a few blocks away. The next day, Blase was back at work at Harkins Builders.

Dawn and Blase on their wedding day

So you might be wondering how they met. Blase owes a debt of gratitude to Uncle Sam and the U.S. Army. Unless he received a deferment, he knew he was going to be drafted because he had a low lottery number. He had actually saved up enough money to afford the tuition to attend a local community college, which may have resulted in a college deferment. Unfortunately, Mom had received an unexpected insurance bill and did not have the money to pay the invoice. Without hesitation, Blase gave her the money, postponed his college education, and soon began his military obligation.

He did his basic training in Ft. Jackson, South Carolina. It's safe to say Blase did not like the military. In fact, after completing basic training, the first thing he did when he came home on leave was to strongly encourage me to sign up for the local Army National Guard unit. I had just finished my junior year at Mt. St. Joe, and at just seventeen years old, the military was the last thing on my mind. But my big brother was watching out for me. By this time, Blase knew he would be doing his advanced infantry training in Ft. Polk, Louisiana. Back then, Fort Polk was known as "Little Vietnam" because of the hot and sticky climate. The rumor was if you went to infantry training at Ft. Polk, your next stop was Vietnam—and in 1966, Vietnam was beginning to escalate. I know he anticipated he would more than likely end up in Vietnam. I ended up getting into the National Guard and avoided Vietnam.

Shortly after arriving home, we went to Benny's Pool Hall with a couple of other friends. Thanks to his construction work and his army training, Blase was now in the best physical shape of his life. During his teenage years, he considered himself a pretty tough guy. He didn't pick a lot of fights, but he certainly didn't back away from them, either. He hung out at pool halls where you would always find an interesting mix of people, including guys who occasionally got into trouble with the law. When we arrived, Blase ran into his friend, Denny, who was playing nine-ball with another person named Herman, who Blase had never met. Denny was losing pretty badly and looking for a way to bow out gracefully, so he suggested that Blase play the guy. Herman, who was playing very well, was eager to engage in a wager with Blase. Sensing Herman's eagerness, Blase negotiated a match in which he would be spotted an additional money ball, giving him a better chance to win. Herman agreed, but only after suggesting that Blase wasn't man enough to play him even up. You can probably tell where this is going. The first game ended very quickly because Blase knocked the nine ball in on the break, which paid double. After Blase won the next two games, Herman got a little more agitated and now wanted to change the terms of the match, which Blase refused to do. At this point, the discussion changed from playing pool to Herman suggesting they go outside and to see how well Blase could fight.

Before Blase could respond, Herman, who was a very strong guy, leaped toward Blase and punched him in the face, knocking him down. As he leaned down to hit him again, I suddenly jumped on Herman's back. As he fell forward, Blase was able to get in a good punch. The next thing I knew, Blase and Herman were both standing up and I was lying on the ground with my arms held tightly around one of Herman's fairly large ankles. With that, the fight stopped long enough for Blase to ask the manager of the pool hall to call the cops. Upon hearing the request, the manager informed Blase that he had just hit a cop. Yes, Herman was a Baltimore City cop. The manager then suggested we call it a day, which we were happy to do.

The next day, our friend John, who had been with us the previous day, walked into the pool hall and immediately saw Herman. He walked up to John and asked him to apologize to Blase. Apparently, Herman had a rough day on the job and decided to take out his frustration on Blase. Of course, Blase hadn't helped matters much. What's really interesting about this story is that soon after this incident, Herman met our sister, Jul, and years later, he became our brother-in-law (for a short period of time).

Blase was not all that excited about going back to the army. When he did return, he endured some interesting challenges during his eight-week advanced training at Fort Polk, most of which came from his drill sergeant. Somehow he got on the wrong side of this guy, and he paid the price for doing so. Every time the drill sergeant needed to demonstrate a hand-to-hand combat move, he always picked Blase. It had gotten to the point where the two of them went behind the barracks to try to settle their differences. It's not that Blase had a big chip on his shoulder, he just didn't like to be bullied by people. He got the crap beat out of him constantly, but he made it through advanced infantry training.

However, instead of going to Vietnam like most of his fellow trainees, Blase had scored well in some of the aptitude tests and was selected to attend military police (MP) school. He performed very well in MP school, graduating ninth in his class of 308 trainees. The top six became honor guards and were sent to Fort McNair in Washington, DC. Blase ended up with more training to become a dog handler and was assigned to a Nike missile base in Franklin Lakes, New Jersey. Apparently, Nike was in the missile business before they got into foot apparel. It turns out that the missile base was a forty-minute drive from Mahwah to Dawn's house in Paterson.

Blase's army picture, 1966

***

They first set eyes on each other on December 9, 1966 at a USO dance somewhere in northern New Jersey. At the time, Dawn worked as a clerk in a lamp factory in Paterson, and some coworkers invited Dawn and her friend to join them. They originally had plans to drive into New York state, where they would be of legal age to consume alcohol. So they decided they would drop by the USO dance for a while, then head north to New York.

Ten girls sat at a large, round table, chatting and listening to music from a DJ, and of course, checking out the men in uniform. Dawn noticed two guys walk into the dance hall, but they were not in uniform. She was immediately attracted to the guy wearing a blue button-down shirt, khaki pants, penny loafers and a fraternity jacket. You might ask why a high school graduate, now in the army, is wearing a fraternity jacket. Isn't that for people who attend college and join fraternities or sororities? In the sixties, in a blue-collar town like Baltimore, "social fraternities" became popular among the smaller communities. And Blase loved his frat jacket. It was silky white with bright green Greek letters. Apparently Dawn liked it, too.

It didn't take very long for Blase and his buddy to make their move on the table of ten lovely ladies. Blase had spotted Dawn as well, and he walked straight up to her and asked her to dance. Dawn had never heard the name Blase, so when he introduced himself, she thought his name was Blake. Blase loved to dance. I think it's how he met girls. I'm sure his strategy was to impress Dawn with his dancing skills, and apparently he accomplished his mission. Their first few dances were fast dances, which then led to slow dances, and by the end of the evening, Blake (I mean Blase) asked Dawn for her phone number. He made his first call to her a week later. In fact, in the days following the initial conversation, they had a number of additional calls, some of which lasted hours, before Blase finally asked her out on a date. When he did ask her out, he started the conversation by saying he had something important he needed to tell her. Dawn's first thought was that he was going to tell her he was married. She was very relieved to hear that they would need to double date because he did not own a car. It should be noted that one of their early dates was going to Sunday Mass.

Isn't it funny how life can change so dramatically and instantly? When you think about it, so many things could have happened that evening which may have resulted in them never even meeting. Blase could have gone to Vietnam or Washington, DC. Dawn could have decided to not go to the USO dance. Blase could have worn his uniform and perhaps Dawn would not have noticed the guy in the frat jacket. Dawn could have said, "No thanks" when asked to dance that evening. It's funny how God works. Many years later, Blase had the opportunity to "pay it forward" to the USO by contributing to the worthy cause and by participating as a member of the Board of Directors for USO Headquarters in Washington, DC. He knew firsthand how the USO helped to boost morale in the military and he never forgot it.

During their courtship, Blase and Dawn would often come to Baltimore for weekend visits and parties. They never came empty-handed, always bringing small gifts and food. In December, 1967, they became engaged, primarily through the strong encouragement of Dawn's mother. She had reminded Blase that if he was going to marry Dawn, he needed to be aware it would take at least a year to make all the arrangements for a proper wedding celebration. When they were not visiting Baltimore, Blase was spending weekends at the Klinger household. It was obvious these two had fallen in love. Dawn and Blase became very close with Dawn's cousin, Bobbie Bridgeman, and his wife, Judy. Like Blase, Bobbie loved golf, and they tried to play as often as they could. They would typically come home after a fun day of golf and start their happy hour with the girls by making them whiskey sours, their drink of choice during those days.

Blase was honorably discharged from the army in May, 1968 and returned to Baltimore. He was able to get his old job back as a construction worker for Southern Engineering, where he worked prior to going into the army. He only worked there for a couple of months, I'm not sure why. He then took a job with Harkins Builders in July, 1968. That was the last job he ever had, and he was there for thirty-nine years.

Blase spent the rest of the summer of '68 working during the week and driving north on I-95 to visit his fiancée on the weekend.

***

A couple of months after moving into their new apartment in Baltimore, Blase handed Dawn the classified section of the *Baltimore Sun* newspaper, a not-so-subtle hint that she might want to consider getting a job. She soon landed a clerical job working for Maryland National Bank in downtown Baltimore. Since they only had the baby blue VW, Dawn took the bus to work every day.

Blase knew he was going to take advantage of the GI Bill and he was anxious to get started. Determined to get his college degree, he enrolled at the University of Baltimore in January of 1969, and spent the next eight years going to night school. He graduated magna cum laude with a bachelor's degree in business. Years later, he became a member of the University of Baltimore Advisory Board.

Shortly after their marriage, Blase and Dawn decided to have children. Unfortunately, Dawn had some difficulties getting pregnant. The thought of not being able to have children was devastating to both of them. They prayed hard for God to bless them with children.

In the fall of 1970, the two-year lease on their apartment was fast approaching, and Blase was doing well at Harkins. He was now a superintendent, and they felt they were ready to purchase their first home. They found a three-bedroom rowhome in a nice neighborhood in Catonsville. The even better news was Dawn became pregnant, and

Jason was born on September 13, 1972, almost four years from the day they were married.

Over the next few years, things continued to go well. Blase and Dawn felt so blessed to have Jason. Having spent years not knowing if they would ever have a child made it even more special for them. Initially, Blase was afraid to even hold Jason. He thought he would break something. He also did not like changing diapers, but eventually learned to do so, thanks to Dawn's strong encouragement. As he began to become more comfortable, he started to do more daring things with little Jason, like tossing him on the bed. Jason loved it. One day, Dawn went to the grocery store and Blase was tossing Jason on the bed when Jason suddenly bit his tongue. Blood was everywhere, and Blase had no clue what to do. In fact, he was so distraught, he stood in the doorway in his underwear in front of all the neighborhood kids waiting for Dawn. Fortunately, she arrived shortly after the accident and all was well. Months went by before Jason was tossed onto the bed again.

Happily, on May 15, 1976, little Brian arrived on the scene. It also happened to be the same week they broke ground on a new home. Blase had continued to progress at Harkins and had received a very nice bonus check, which he immediately invested in a 2.5-acre lot in a development called Woodmark in Howard County. Since Blase was his own general contractor, and since he knew a lot of folks in the construction industry, he was able to complete the four-bedroom home in September, 1976, just four months after breaking ground.

It was good that Blase and Dawn decided on a four-bedroom house because not long after they moved into their new home, and much to their surprise, Dawn unexpectedly became pregnant again. So the following September, just sixteen months after Brian was born, little Kevin arrived on September 8, 1977.

A beautiful home, a beautiful wife, and three adorable little boys, life doesn't get any better than this. In the early years, summer vacations were spent at the beach in Ocean City, Maryland with family and friends. As the children grew up, Blase always found time to coach his boys in basketball and baseball in the Howard County Youth League. When the kids were little, Blase would have them wear hard hats, and he would take them on his job sites on Saturdays and "put them to work." They also started a birthday tradition where they would take each son out to a special dinner to celebrate each of their birthdays, just Mom, Dad, and the birthday boy. The boys enjoyed these celebrations so much that the tradition continued into adulthood and eventually included their spouses.

Goofy, Blase, and Kevin on a family trip to Disney World in 1982

Family Picture, 1990

My Brother, My Keeper

The boys grew up attending St. Louis Catholic Grade School, then moved on to Mt. St. Joseph High School, the same school Blase was unable to attend when he was growing up. There is no question Blase lived vicariously through his boys. Both Jason and Brian played football and lacrosse, and Kevin played golf. When Blase went to high school, his extracurricular activities included delivering newspapers, slinging hamburgers, and caddying at the country club, but he loved watching his boys grow up in an environment that he was unable to. He did everything in his power to attend and cheer at every event he possibly could, and it was rare that he missed one. What a thrill for Blase and what a great thrill for his boys.

After graduating from Mt. St. Joe, Jason and Brian attended the University of Delaware and Kevin attended Western Maryland College. They all graduated with degrees and are now making their mark on the world.

On September 22, 2007, Dawn and Blase celebrated their thirty-ninth wedding anniversary quietly at home after returning from University of Maryland Hospital, where he had just completed a liver procedure three days before. It was just ten days before he died. Fortunately for them, they had so many wonderful memories to share—from memorable trips to Italy, Germany, Greece, Tahiti, Puerto Rico, and many other places over the years—to just babysitting their four wonderful grandchildren whom they cherish so much. Life had been very good for this couple who met and fell for each other at a USO dance over forty years ago, and they were both grateful for all the blessings bestowed on them over those years.

Memorandum

To: All Personnel

From: Blase Cooke

Re: THOUGHTS FOR THE DAY

"Be patient with everyone, but above all, with yourself."

"Charity is an ascending humility, and humility is a descending charity."

"The business of finding fault is very easy, and that of doing better very difficult."

"The well-being of a household depends on the parents' words, but far more on their behavior."

"We must love our friends notwithstanding their imperfections, but we must not love their imperfections."

"The crosses that we shape for ourselves are always lighter than the ones laid upon us."

"We must be prepared to see weeds growing in our garden and also have the courage to pull them out."

"Blessed are the hearts which can bend; they shall never be broken."

"One kind word wins more willing service than a hundred harsh orders or stern reproofs."

"Bearing with the imperfections of our neighbor is one of the chief characteristics of our love for him."

Chapter 4

Family Fun at Gratitude Farm—Sykesville, MD, September 2, 2007

"This is a testament of the love that is shared
For the one who gives so much and who unselfishly cares.
I'm sure your mom and dad are filled with joy
To know the world's a better place because of their little boy!
A special thank you from the lives that you touch.
We all want to thank you so very much.
With love, your godson, John."

Blase's Fiftieth Birthday Celebration – John Young, Jr., February 3, 1997

It was Sunday, September 2, 2007, exactly one month before Blase would die, and it would be the last time he ever saw Gratitude Farm. The event was a birthday celebration for Blase and Dawn's two youngest grandchildren, Sofi and Reeves, who were celebrating their second birthdays. There were perhaps fifty family and friends attending, and it was a truly beautiful day.

Blase and family members at Gratitude Farm, September 2, 2007

In 2003, Blase purchased a piece of property about ten minutes from his home called Gratitude Farm. It's a beautiful and tranquil sixty-acre farm with two homes, a couple of barns, and a lovely little lake. He had been looking for a piece of property like this for quite a while. A couple of months prior to finding Gratitude Farm, he had made an offer on another piece of property, but the deal did not happen. It turned out to be a blessing in disguise because when he saw this property, he knew immediately it was perfect.

One of the reasons Blase purchased Gratitude Farm was to have a place for outdoor events for family and friends, just like the one we were celebrating that Sunday afternoon in September. He wanted to continue the family tradition, which started back in the early seventies when he and our family would visit our cousins, Bill and Bernice Young, for the annual family reunion. Bill and Bernice lived with their four children in a house in Arbutus, Maryland, located in southwest Baltimore. Bill, who was an electrician by trade, built an in-ground pool in the backyard, and every summer, he and Bernice would throw a party and invite family and friends. The party would start in the early afternoon and last late into the evening. Bill and Bern would supply the beer, burgers, and dogs, while every family would bring the rest of the feast, which included assorted drinks, salads, side dishes, and, of course, desserts. In addition to the pool, we would toss horseshoes and participate in other outdoor games. As the day moved into the evening and the music got louder, singing and dancing would be a part of the fun as well. The annual event continued at Bill and Bern's house for many years.

Below is one of John Young's recollections he verbally shared with me regarding a prank from Blase during one of the reunions. John is the "baby boy" in the Young family. He is also Blase's godson.

During one of the family reunions, John was working at the local gas station, so he was not able to attend. He decided to stop by on his lunch hour to say hi to everyone and have a *couple of burgers. He had about $600 dollars in his pocket and he was dressed in his gas station uniform. He was hanging out at the pool and all of the sudden, Blase snuck up on him and whispered in John's ear "I've got you now." He told John that he would let him go if he said, "Please Blase, let me go." Before he could get all the words out of his mouth, he was in the water, uniform, money, and all. A short while later, he was back at the gas station in his soaking wet uniform, handing out wet dollar bills to his customers. He didn't tell me how he explained the situation to his customers and I didn't ask.*

John went on to say that after he married his wife, Robin, and they started a family, every Christmas they would receive a gift card from Blase and Dawn. John was very appreciative and wanted to take Blase out to lunch to thank him for his generosity. When he went to his office, Blase suggested they have lunch and a talk in Blase's office. He was very surprised to learn that Blase very often had lunch in his office. He would buy sliced turkey from the local deli and make his own sandwich and eat at his desk. He often had these working lunches with employees, friends, and family members. He was more productive that way, and he always remembered everything you said and would follow up on any action items that would come out of those luncheon meetings. John always had the comfort that if he ever needed anything, Blase would be there for him.

As we grew older, got married, and had our own families, the number of attendees increased and eventually we outgrew the Young's home in Arbutus. Initially, John and Robin took over hosting the event for a few years at their home in Carroll County. Then the reunion venue was moved to the home of the oldest Young daughter, Diana, and her husband, Kenny, who still host the annual event at their home in

Carroll County, Maryland. Now our children's children are enjoying the fun and getting to know their distant cousins. There were some in-between years where my sister, Aggie, and cousin, Eileen, coordinated the reunion at a commercial facility called Lake Cascade.

***

In 1979, my bride, Wanda, and our three little children moved to northern Virginia for a new job opportunity in the Washington, DC area. It was tough leaving our family and friends in Baltimore. In reality, we never left them because we were constantly going back for holidays, baby showers, weddings, dinner parties, sporting events, etc.; you name it, and we were in the car. Since we were the ones who moved away, we realized we would need to make the sacrifice, but it wasn't much of a sacrifice since we really enjoyed being with our families anyway.

In the mid-eighties, after settling into a larger home, we decided to come up with an annual event where we would invite our family and friends to make the trek to Virginia for a get-together. You need to understand that most people who are born and raised in Baltimore typically stay in Baltimore. In many cases, when they grow into adulthood and get married, they don't wander very far away from the neighborhoods in which they originally grew up, so the idea of attending a family event would not normally include a long drive, (assuming one would call a one-hour drive long). Plus the notion of traveling to another state for most Baltimoreans is like going to another country, so we really needed to come up with an attractive offering that would entice people to come. Knowing we had a very competitive group of family and friends we came up with the idea of the Family Olympics. And, of course, the inspiration for even having an event like this came from Bill and Bernice Young and those wonderful get-togethers we experienced in our younger years. I'm sure at the time, they had no idea of the incredibly positive impact they were having on our entire family, and we are all so grateful for the wonderful and positive affect they had on our lives and our families.

Over the course of the next fifteen years, we hosted the Family Olympics at our home. Every year, we developed competitive events, established teams, and would spend the next four to six hours competing our hearts out to win the gold medal. We typically had anywhere from seventy-five to ninety people show up, and their ages ranged from a few months to over eighty years, and just about everyone participated in at least one event. On the day of the event, captains would be selected, then teams would be drafted. We had some basic rules, like no immediate family members could be on the same team. We also encouraged fun, fairness, and sportsmanship, although given the competitive nature of many of the participants, that was sometimes a challenge, but an enjoyable one. We would typically have between six or seven events, including events like the peanut toss, three-legged relay race, water balloon toss, bubble gum blowing (mostly younger kids), and the infamous "orange pass" (see below for some details). At the end of the competition, we would eat and laugh, talk and laugh, and sing and dance, just like the old days at Bill and Bern's.

The Blaser and Billy competing in the Marshmallow relay race, 1995

65

Phil Cooke

Below is the invitation to our last Family Olympics event held in 2004.

TO: *Family Olympics Participants*

FROM: *President, Chairman, & CEO of the International Family Olympics World Foundation (IFOWF (pronounced if-off)*

SUBJECT: *2004 FAMILY OLYMPICS – The Passing of the Torch*

It is with a sense of excitement and melancholy that we announce our Final Family Olympics from the Cookes of Virginia. You might ask why? Why now? What's up with this? What in the %#&$%* is going on here? Well, to get the answer, you are just going to have to show up for the event. And I can guarantee you won't regret it.

This year, the Olympics will take place on Saturday, October 16, beginning promptly at 2:00 PM at the Cookes of Virginia. Please RSVP by October 1. We would appreciate it if each family could bring a salad, appetizer, or dessert, plus some non-alcoholic drinks. We will provide the beer, wine, and meat (and a hearty bowl of soup). Please contact my gorgeous assistant, Wanda, to let her know what you plan to bring.

This year, the games will start with the grand opening ceremony, "Parade of Families." We are asking each family to bring their family coat of arms (you know, like a flag), on a pole (you know, like a flag pole), and have your most athletic family member hold the pole. In order for you to participate in the "hold the pole" ceremony you must arrive by 2:00 p.m., so be prompt. Please make sure you choose your pole holder carefully and that your designated pole holder holds his/her pole properly. Who knows? Maybe the best pole holder will win a gold pole for the best pole holder, and who also knows? Maybe that best pole holder can trade in that gold pole for a gold medal, and maybe that gold medal winner will end up on my team. Ha-ha!

I thought I would close this letter with some thoughts on what the Family Olympics has meant to me, your IFOWF Chairman through the years.

What the Family Olympics mean to me

O – O is for the orange pass. I don't think the Family Olympics would have had as much meaning if it wasn't for the orange pass. If you think about it, some of us got to know family members in a way we otherwise never would have. I'll never forget the bear hug that Greg Cooke put on Tom Hasslebein in '98, and then the time that Jim McGinnis fell asleep while passing the orange to Shannon Conroy and almost suffocated her.

L – L is for the laughter and love shared before, during, and after the events. (On second thought, let's just leave it at before and during the events.) Remember "card sucking," karaoke, jump rope (when Colleen got shot), the "spin around the bat" relay race, and the water balloon toss? Remember when my porch sank during the family and friends photo? Boy, that was a hoot!

Y – Y is for Karaoke. (I couldn't think of a good Y word.) Will we ever again hear Bernice sing "A Horse With No Name" the way she sang that night back in 1997? By the way, Bernice was awarded a special gold medal by the IFOWF for her incredible performance that night.

Phil Cooke

M – M is for mojo. Please bring your MoJo with you again this year. As you know, no one is allowed to participate unless his/her mojo is fully operational.

P – P is for all the participants of the Family Olympics over the years, especially those of you who were not able to experience "winning the gold," but we all know what's really important is participation, right?

I – I is for inspiration. How many times were you inspired by a teammate or fellow competitor? Okay, maybe not so many times. But the food and the company were really great!

C – C is for competition. Yes, every year, everyone put every ounce of effort he or she had onto the field. Regardless if you won or lost, you can always tell your grandkids you made the effort, and we have the pictures to prove it.

S – S is for spirit. Whether you got two or six peanuts in the cup, whether you made two or ten baskets, whether you blew the biggest bubble, or whether you scratched on the eight-ball to lose the pool tournament gold medal (I won't mention a name here because it's too painful), each and every one of the participants exhibited unyielding spirit. Your spirit is what I will take with me from these games (along with my many gold medals).

And that, my friends and family, is what the Family Olympics mean to me. With all due respect to the recently ended games in Greece, I think our events and participants exemplify the Olympic spirit to the fullest extent.

We hope y'all can make it down this year, and we look forward to seeing you.

The Cooke Family of Virginia

A typical Family Olympics gathering in the mid-nineties

By the time we completed that last Family Olympics in Virginia in 2004, Blase had purchased Gratitude Farm. One of his dreams was that the farm would become a gathering place for the next generation of our family and friends to continue the tradition that started many years ago by Bill and Bernice. The good news is that his dream is being fulfilled. The farm has been the site of many memorable events over the past few years, and I'm sure it will continue to be a wonderful gathering place for generations to come.

Phil Cooke

Below is a special memory experienced by Blase and Kim Vicchio at Gratitude Farm. Kim's husband Rocco had fallen off a roof a few years back and had become paralyzed. As a result of some very determined and painful physical therapy, Rocco beat the odds and was able to walk again. In late 2005, when Blase began having difficulty walking, both Rocco and Kim were there to help in any way they could. I know Blase had a very special bond with them. I remember a conversation we had about how impressed he was with Rocco during his recovery period, particularly with how he handled the pain and how he never complained. Blase also told me how much Kim and Rocco helped him with their positive attitudes and encouragement.

Email from Kim Vicchio, February 13, 2008

Of course, the thing I will remember about Blase was how thoughtful he was of others, even in the midst of his own battle with cancer. One of my favorite memories of Blase was the night spent at the farm having a weenie roast. Blase was wrapped up in blankets, sitting by the fire, and we were singing songs. He was laughing because I had so many songs I knew from teaching kindergarten. We were laughing because I kept rubbing his legs and hands to keep him warm and he had that little embarrassed boyish grin on his face and said, "That feels so good." We were all lightheartedly complaining about getting old and how stiff we were in the mornings, especially Rocco. Blase asked if we had ever tried magnets. I said that we had bought some magnet inserts for Rocco's shoes a few years back. We were laughing because Roc said, "Yeah, I might be a lot worse off without them!" A few weeks later, a big package arrived at the door. I hadn't ordered anything, so I couldn't imagine what it could be. There inside was a queen-size magnetic mattress pad from Blase with a note that said, "I hope this helps, Rocco, love Blase."

70

Blase was the most grateful person I have ever known, and Gratitude Farm would have been the perfect place for Blase and Dawn to grow old along with family and friends. We used to talk about sitting in rocking chairs in our nineties, reflecting upon all the wonderful experiences we enjoyed over the course of our lives. The good news for Blase is he hardly ever wasted any of the time he had on this Earth. He raised a beautiful family, he ran a successful business, he gave back to those in need, and he took time to have a whole lot of fun along the way. The Thought for the Day that follows seems to be a fitting ending to this chapter.

Memorandum

To: All Employees

From: Blase Cooke

Re: THOUGHT FOR THE DAY

---

*The message below was forwarded to me by a good friend.
EVERYONE should read this to his or her friends, family, etc.
It should make us all appreciate what we have.*

Imagine . . .

*There is a bank that credits your account each morning with
$86,400. It carries over no balance from day to day. Every evening
deletes whatever part of the balance you failed to use during the day.
What would you do? Draw out ALL OF IT, of course!*

*Each of us has such a bank. Its name is TIME. Every morning,
it credits you with 86,400 seconds. Every night it writes off, as lost,
whatever of this you have failed to invest to good purpose. It carries
over no balance. It allows no overdraft.*

*Each day, it opens a new account for you. Each night, it burns the
remains of the day. If you fail to use the day's deposits, the loss
is yours.*

*There is no going back. There is no drawing against the "tomorrow."
You must live in the present on today's deposits. Invest it so as to get
from it the utmost in health, happiness, and success! The clock is
running. Make the most of today.*

My Brother, My Keeper

To realize the value of ONE YEAR,
ask a student who failed a grade.

To realize the value of ONE MONTH,
ask a mother who gave birth to a premature baby.

To realize the value of ONE WEEK,
ask the editor of a weekly newspaper.

To realize the value of ONE HOUR,
ask the lovers who are waiting to meet.

To realize the value of ONE MINUTE,
ask a person who missed the train.

To realize the value of ONE SECOND,
ask a person who just avoided an accident.

To realize the value of ONE MILLISECOND,
ask the person who won a silver medal in the Olympics.

Treasure every moment that you have! And treasure it more because you shared it with someone special, special enough to spend your time.

And remember that time waits for no one. Yesterday is history. Tomorrow is a mystery. Today is a gift. That's why it's called the present!

Friends are a very rare jewel, indeed. They make you smile and encourage you to succeed. They lend an ear, they share a word of praise, and they always want to open their hearts to us.

Chapter 5

Harkins Builders, Inc.—December 22, 2006

". . . that folder was a constant in his life to the day he died . . ."

Brian Cooke's Eulogy, October 5, 2007

Friday, December 22, 2006 was the last day Blase would ever spend in his office at Harkins Builders. I can only guess that he didn't know it at the time, or perhaps he did. We will never know. It was the last workday before the Christmas holiday. He had asked Jason to drive him to the office so he could attend the company's annual Christmas party. By this time, he was completely paralyzed from the waist down and relegated to a wheelchair. He was able to get around thanks to a handicapped accessible van they had recently acquired, but it was quite an effort. Although he was not feeling very well, he still wanted to at least make an appearance at the party to wish everyone a joyful and peaceful holiday season. Before leaving, he asked Jason to wheel him up to his second floor office. He and Dawn would be leaving in early January to fly to their winter home in Fort Myers, Florida, so it's possible he wanted to gather up some materials to take with him, although when he left the office, he did not take anything. He knew he would be in Florida for a number of months because he was scheduled to begin a long stint of chemotherapy at the Moffitt Cancer Research Center in Tampa. My sense is that he just simply missed being there. He loved Harkins, he loved being their leader, and I'm sure he longed for things to return to the way they used to be. Maybe, at some level, he knew he would never be back.

Blase's office was filled with, among other things, pictures, plaques, awards, books, and motivational tapes. He loved to share what he had learned from those books and tapes. In short, his office was a microcosm of most of his life, right there for everyone to see. He was in his thirty-ninth year at Harkins Builders. His office offered a lucid picture of his balanced lifestyle between work and family, his accomplishments, and the rewards and recognition which came from those accomplishments. What was really unique about Blase was his inherent desire to share what made him successful with others. As you read this today, Blase's office is pretty much the same as it was on the last day he spent there in 2006.

***

Thomas P. Harkins, Inc. was founded by Tom Harkins in 1965. In May, 1968, after an honorable discharge from the U.S. Army, Blase joined the company as a laborer earning three dollars an hour. He rose steadily through the ranks working in a number of different field positions including site manager, finish superintendent, and project manager. Below is a recollection from one of Blase's first supervisors, Ted Nelson, who worked with Blase at the start of his career at Harkins and retired as the vice-president of estimating after almost forty years of service.

> *"Blase was willing to do anything that was best for the company. I was a project manager for the Sumner Village project and Blase was site manager for the community building—his first assignment as a site manager. I was having trouble getting units turned over, and I asked Blase if he would be my finish superintendent for the units. He immediately said, yes, and within a short period of time, had the production turned around and turnovers to the owner completed. Blase was also able to make very tough business decisions that some individuals did not like, but were in the best interest of the company. He was a good businessman, but most of all, he was a good person and a great friend."*

My Brother, My Keeper

After ten years of primarily working field jobs, Blase was promoted to division manager in 1978, vice president in 1980, executive vice president of construction in 1982, and president and chief operating officer in May, 1984. Over the next ten years, Tom and Blase worked very closely together, and their leadership led Harkins Builders to becoming, not only one of the largest construction firms in the mid-Atlantic region, but more importantly, one of the most respected and high-quality construction firms in the industry as well. Below is how Gary Garafolo, the current chief financial officer for Harkins, reflected on his long-term relationship with both Tom and Blase.

Tom and Blase shared the vision that Harkins Builders would not only be an exceptional builder with a commitment to excellence for its clients, but also a corporate civic leader that gave its time and money to help those less fortunate or in need.

Whether he was working on a business venture or on any of the numerous charitable causes he led, it was Blase's passion for excellence and a desire to create the best possible outcome for all parties involved that I believe set him apart from other leaders. It was never enough to just be involved. If a project was going to have his name on it, it would have to live up to the rigorous standards he set for himself and the people involved. Setbacks were going to happen, and were even acceptable, but failure was not.

In business, Blase combined this passion with a straightforward philosophy: find the best employees, give them everything they need to be successful, including a share of the profits they generate, and let them do their job. He was a great believer that if employees shared in the profits they generated, then the employees' and the company's interests were the same, which was a win-win for both parties.

77

As Blase's business ventures expanded, his leadership and management style became his biggest strength. In his interactions with employees in the office or on the site visits he made to each of our projects, he possessed the ability to bring people together to focus on one common goal. In either venue, Blase was a firm believer that the person most able to make the proper decision wasn't him, but rather, the employees closest to the decision. Blase was always available to offer his advice, but the decision was theirs to make. If a bad decision was made, he would not second guess it, but he did insist on everyone involved in that decision understanding what went wrong and how they could learn from their mistake. This style helped create a culture of trust and loyalty, which resulted in a substantially higher employee retention rate than is typically seen in the construction industry. Blase felt strongly that Harkins' most valuable asset was the talent of its employees, and he firmly believed the retention of those employees, whether an entry level person just starting in the field or an executive, led to stability. This, in turn, led to sustainable long-term growth and profitability for the company and its employees.

Blase in his office at Harkins Builders

**Dawn and Blase sharing a dance
at a company event**

Although Blase spent over twenty-eight of his thirty-eight years
working as an executive, he never lost his appreciation and respect for
all the employees who worked so hard in the field. In fact, he felt one
of his most important roles in the company was to get out and visit as
many people as he could on the job sites. A great example of how
Blase appreciated and treated all of his employees was how he dealt
with newly hired field employees, like Brendan, who met Blase in
November, 2004, at a company meeting:

> *I was just a nineteen-year old boy at the time I first met Blase.
> I had just recently joined the Harkins Builders family as my first
> full-time career-oriented job. Within a month of employment,
> Blase was holding the annual State of the Company meeting. At
> the end of the meeting, Blase recognized a few new employees to
> the company, including myself, and asked for all the new*

employees to meet with him for a quick exchange of words and a formal introduction. At the time, I recognized only a handful of faces and knew even less people by name. I walked up to Blasé, and after a brief introduction, he proceeded to ask about my family. To my amazement, Blase knew my entire family by name. Blase, a man I had just met for the first time, was asking me, "How is your sister, Kellie, doing, and how does she like her new school? How are your parents, Maureen and Joseph, doing?" He had taken the time out of his extremely busy day to get to know me and my family. Never before and never again since have I ever seen any individual in the work force genuinely care about another person. Blase was a man blessed with an extraordinary gift for caring, a characteristic I will always strive to mimic.

It's very ironic that Tom Harkins also suffered for approximately six years with a debilitating illness before his death in 1993. In Tom's case, he was diagnosed with leukemia in the latter part of 1987. Shortly after Tom's death, Blase assumed full ownership of the company, and was elected chairman and CEO of Harkins Builders, Inc. in August, 1993. Through his tremendous leadership, great community involvement, and charitable giving, Blase built on the foundation Mr. Harkins had established, sustaining the company's reputation and leading Harkins Builders to even greater success and prosperity. One of his most significant legacies is the employee stock ownership plan, which he created as a retirement vehicle for Harkins employees, who are now the majority owners of the company.

In September, 1999, an article written by Edwards Holliday entitled, "CEO Cooke Succeeds Through Personal Leadership," appeared in a local business magazine. The tagline of the story was that Blase had essentially become the rags-to-riches Horatio Alger story for the construction industry. My favorite quote from the story centered on Blase's approach to living every day without regret because of three uncompromising beliefs: "Take good care of yourself spiritually and physically, do everything in moderation, and use good judgment." Like many people Blase had met, Mr. Holliday also had been touched in a special way, as evidenced by his beautiful letter he wrote the day after Blase died.

October 3, 2007

Dear All at Harkins Builders and the Cooke Family,

I feel for you over the loss of your beloved J.P. Blase Cooke. Please find enclosed a donation to My Brother's Keeper in his name.

May he be rejoicing with his Creator and smiling upon you. May the love that Blase brought into our world be multiplied by the thousands of lives that he has touched.

To say that he was a great man just isn't enough.

Blase had a profound impact on my life, as he has had on many, many others, and I will miss him dearly.

He stood for all of the things that really make a man: faithful, committed, determined, passionate, hard worker, servant's heart, family first, philanthropic, generous, competitive, goal-setter, team player, honest, straight shooter, humble, and respectful.

Blase, more than anyone I know, was master of his attitude—no matter what. He demonstrated what it means to take personal responsibility for one's life.

When I interviewed Blase for the article that ran in The Business Monthly, *September, 1999, I knew immediately that he was the kind of CEO who walked his talk and truly cared about his employees, family, community, and friends. He so embodied the spirit and principles that we espouse in our client work that I titled his article "Cooke Succeeds Through Personal Leadership," because our core personal development program is called Effective Personal Leadership, and he was the closest person I ever interviewed that deserved that title association. Before I left his office on the day of the interview, he opened up a huge file drawer and invited me to borrow any recording from his massive positive thinking library. That was impressive, because most of the items were virtually worn out from use—his use.*

Blase was a model leader, and he will forever hold a special place in my mind and heart.

Blessings to Blase, to you, and to your families.

Best regards,

Edwards A. Holliday
President

***

As mentioned earlier, one of Blase's greatest strengths was his ability and desire to surround himself with great people, and he had a very large number of talented and dedicated employees at Harkins. Perhaps one of his most important hires over the years was Joani Van Tuyl, his administrative assistant for twenty-five years. Joani started working for Blase on Monday, October 4, 1982. At the time, Blase was the executive vice president of construction and the number two guy in the company.

My Brother, My Keeper

Joani has three vivid memories of her early days at Harkins. The first was the interview with Blase itself. Joani had already interviewed with Gladys, who had been Tom Harkins' longtime administrative assistant, and she knew she wanted the job. At the time, Joani was twenty-four years old and worked as an administrative assistant for a government contractor. This was the only job she had ever had, and she never had to interview for it. Since this was her first ever formal interview, and since she was interviewing to work directly for an executive in the company, she was extremely nervous, and she was even more nervous when she arrived for the interview because she was ten minutes late. The interview with Blase lasted only twenty minutes and Joani was offered the job the same day. I suspect the real interview occurred in the initial meeting with Gladys because Blase knew she was a great employee, and I'm sure he realized that Gladys knew what Blase needed more so than he did himself. Blase just confirmed her recommendation. The best news of all was that Gladys was right and Blase found an indispensable employee and lifelong friend.

Joani's next vivid memory occurred two days after she started her job when she met Dawn, who "just happened to be in the neighborhood" and dropped by to say hi. According to Joani, she thought Dawn had come by to "check her out." Well, needless to say, they hit it off immediately and their close relationship continues to this day. Within thirty days into the job, Blase asked Joani to begin handling the family's personal finances, and since the very beginning, Joani quickly became an integral part of Blase's business and his family's life.

Joani's last, and very touching early memory occurred in 1984 when she told Blase that her son, Kelly, was scheduled to go into the hospital to have tubes put in his ears. Blase simply said, "I'll say a prayer for him." No one had ever said that to Joani and his sincere and kind expression has always stayed with her.

Joani celebrated her twenty-five year anniversary at Harkins on October 4, 2007, just two days after Blase passed away. She had written the note below a couple of weeks before, but had not delivered it until a few days before he died. Blase read Joani's note on Monday, October 1, 2007, the day before he died.

Dear Blase:

As my twenty-fifth anniversary with you and Harkins Builders approaches, I wanted to share a few memories and some very important lessons YOU have taught me over the years.

Twenty-five years—I still remember my interview with you and leaving after my first day thinking, "What have I gotten myself into?" I have to admit, at first, you scared me a little. You did everything fast—talked, walked, drove, and it took some getting used to. Then, after about three weeks, something clicked—I wasn't scared anymore and I knew I was where I was supposed to be.

Because of you, I have been able to experience things I never would have otherwise—our trip to Palm Springs because you won "Entrepreneur of the Year," meeting President Bush and three governors, and sharing family weddings across the country.

Working with you has been a learning experience every day. You always challenge me to do my best, and for that, I will be forever grateful. Some of the greatest lessons I have learned from you are:

1. Make time for what's important, especially family
2. Be firm, but fair
3. Treat everyone well and the same

4. *Work hard, play hard (but not too hard)*
5. *Take some risk*
6. *Have a plan*
7. *Have faith, pray*
8. *"Terrific" is a state of mind*
9. *Write thank you notes*
10. *Set goals*
11. *Never, ever give up on something or someone you believe in*
12. *Use good judgment, do everything in moderation, and take good care of yourself, both spiritually and physically*

And you have taught me all of this and more just by being you—Blase. You lead by example—another valuable lesson.

I am grateful every day that I have the chance to work with and learn from you. Thank you for taking a chance on me.

I admire you, respect you and love you. Happy anniversary to us!

Love,

Joani

Blase and Joani, 2007

Phil Cooke

I can't talk about Blase and Harkins Builders without mentioning the "folder." Tom Harkins had instituted a practice where he would collect every piece of correspondence related to the construction business and its clients into a reading file, which he would review on a weekly basis. This essentially included any correspondence which went out to or was received from a Harkins client. When Blase became executive vice president of Harkins, he had responsibility across the entire organization. He quickly realized the importance of this practice, and began reviewing this file as well. Blase never took the time to review this information in the office because he was typically interacting face-to-face with employees, clients, and others in meetings, phone calls, and site visits. This reading file was put into the "folder," and it left an indelible mark on Blase's family because the folder was always somewhere near him. Like Tom did before him, Blase wanted to be aware, in advance, of what was going on with his clients. He wanted no surprises, and he wanted to be prepared to address issues in a proactive and timely manner.

As the cancer progressed and kept Blase away from the office more and more, Joani would bring the folder to Blase twice a week. Now it included even more items which required his attention or approval. When he was away in Florida, the folder was simply put into Fed-Ex packages and delivered to him. I saw his folder as one of the secrets to his success. It enabled him to keep his life in balance while still being a very effective leader. In fact, he was pulling papers from his folder right until the day before he died.

Throughout Blase's career at Harkin's, he developed a significant number of deep personal friendships that originally began as a business relationship. Below is just one of the many examples of these incredible friendships that developed—this one with Bill Franey, who gave the following eulogy at Blase's funeral. The only reference to his business relationship with Blase is to explain how they originally met.

My Brother, My Keeper

October 5, 2007—Bill Franey's Eulogy to Blase

I'm grateful for the opportunity to speak today in celebration of the life of Blase Cooke. I will attempt to convey to you my personal relationship and feelings with this wonderful human being. Like all of you present today, we have been graced and touched by one extraordinary individual. Many of us here today, including me, would consider Blase our best friend. He was truly a special person in my life.

I first met Blase in the early '80s in conjunction with a business relationship I had with Harkins Builders.

It wasn't until several years later that I got to really know Blase. The event that was the catalyst was a lacrosse game at Mt. St. Joe High School where Jason and my son, Ryan, were competing against each other. It was at this game that Blase and I first connected on a personal level, and I learned some of the essence of the man. During the game, I learned how important his family was to him, especially his bride, Dawn, and their three sons Jason, Kevin, and Brian, and how proud he was of his family.

Over the ensuing months and years, a portrait of Blase developed in my mind. This portrait showed a man that put family first, was deeply religious, intelligent, passionate, competitive, optimistic, compassionate, focused, humble, and who was goal-oriented. He was also the strongest-willed person that I have ever encountered. Blase was stubborn, a trait we shared together that I have always claimed was a genetic defect of the Irish. Although Blase was competitive in business and very successful in that endeavor, he was really competitive when it came to golf and other games.

We played in many golf tournaments together, and on the first tee, he would take control; he was our captain and coach. He would set a goal for the team as to how many under par we needed to WIN. He would also say this is the best team he had ever played on. He was usually right about the number, and on more occasions than not, we would win. Blase was a very focused individual, and he used to say if you were going to play, you may as well play to win.

On the passionate and stubborn side, I can remember a trip to Bermuda. The group was sitting at a table at the hotel, and Blase was having a passionate discussion, when all of a sudden, he stopped and apologized to the group. My wife then told Blase that it was okay to be passionate, and that gave him the license to continue. He asked for forgiveness and instead got permission, and he took advantage of it.

I have Blase to thank for many things, but two that stand out are my involvement with Catholic Charities and the Archdiocese of Baltimore over the last twenty years. This involvement has broadened my horizons with respect to those in need, and I think it has made me a better person.

Blase also invited me to participate in the building of My Brother's Keeper in his boyhood neighborhood in Irvington. Through his dedication working with Father Mike Murphy, Dave Carney, and others, and with Joani as the organizer, the Blase Cooke Center is now a reality and will continue to serve the poor of that area for many years to come. Blase, I can never thank you enough for these great experiences.

Blase was also a humanitarian and philanthropist who gave his time and money to many projects in the area, too numerous to mention all of them.

We also shared a great love for the Emerald Isle and went there many times over the years to play golf. The players were somewhat different each time, but the theme was the same; he kept the daily scoring tabs on a special sheet, which no one could decipher, and he would tell us on the bus after golf where we stood. All the players had to do was send in a check, show up on time for the plane, and on arrival, get in the bus to play golf. He had, through Joani, taken care of all of the arrangements, and the players could just have fun.

I remember one night in Tralee, after we finished dinner, a card game ensued. Blase was in the game, but he set a limit that he would stop playing at 11:00 p.m. so that he could call Dawn and then get some sleep. His timing was impeccable because at five minutes to eleven, he had everyone's money and left to call his bride. This was vintage Blase. If you say you're going to do something, then just do it.

Blase was truly a man with the right priorities in life, with family first and his strong religious commitment that gave him comfort through his life. Through the many years of friendship, whenever we talked or met privately, he would always end the conversation with the words, "I will keep you in my prayers." THAT MADE HIM A SPECIAL PERSON TO ME.

Blase's work is done, but I'm sure he is already involved with something in Heaven. That was his nature. He will be missed by all of us, but not forgotten. I love you, Blase, and I will miss you.

***

Although Blase's last day in his office occurred on December 22, 2006, very much like his father before him, he literally worked until the day before he died. You see, when Joani stopped by the Tuesday before Blase passed, she didn't just bring him her letter, she brought him the folder, full of emails, memos, financial reports, etc. It was a compilation of all the important activities going on at Harkins for the previous week that may or may not have needed Blase's attention, but Blase was still the CEO, and he still believed he would recover from the cancer, so he kept on doing what he had always done. He worked.

How many people do you know who were literally on their deathbeds going through a folder of mostly work-related information? The truth of the matter is Blase was so weak, he didn't really read much of anything that day. What's important is that Blase kept trying, kept fighting, and would not give up, even until his last day.

Memorandum

To: Thought For The Day Recipients

From: Blase Cooke

Re: HOW TO CREATE THE TEAM NO ONE CAN BEAT

Whatever the industry, its great leaders share basic qualities. In his book, Think Like a Champion: Building Success One Victory at a Time, *Denver Broncos coach Mike Shanahan shares his insight into the principles of creating a winning team on or in any field.*

Here is Shanahan's fifteen-point game plan for winning teams:

1. *Team matters more than individuals.*
2. *Every job is important.*
3. *Treat everyone with respect.*
4. *Share both victories and defeats.*
5. *Accept criticism.*
6. *Keep the boss well-informed.*
7. *Focus on your work ethic, not others'.*
8. *Allow for difference in lifestyle.*
9. *Be more creative than predictable.*
10. *Let go of failed ideas.*
11. *Employ structure and order.*
12. *Reward those who produce.*
13. *Find different ways to motivate your employees.*
14. *Keep your employees fresh.*
15. *Protect your system.*

Thanks to Larry Kraemer for submitting this Thought For the Day.

Chapter 6

Jason and Alexis' Wedding
St. Ignatius Church—Baltimore, MD
November 2, 2000

"I ask that we all try to fill this void by honoring Blase, living each day with the same passion, faith, and enthusiasm that he did, staying together as one large family, helping others in need, volunteering our time and money, raising our children with lots of love and attention and remembering the good times . . ."

Jason Cooke Eulogy – October 5, 2007

There was never a question in Jason's mind about who would be his best man for his wedding—his dad. There was also never a question the wedding would be held in a Catholic church and there would be a full Mass celebrated. Jason knew how proud it would make Blase feel, and he always strived to make his dad proud. If you asked Blase his greatest accomplishment in life, he would have told you, without question, it was his family. That's what life was all about for Blase. It's clear from his best man toast below how proud he was to have been selected to be Jason's best man.

As you can imagine, I am really quite honored to be the best man in Jason and Alexis' wedding. Actually, for many years, I have been trying to convince Dawn that I am the best man, but today, there is no doubt about it. You may know that Irish people have a tendency to be red-faced. The truth of the matter is that they are very happy people and the happier they are, the redder their complexion.

Phil Cooke

I would very much like to welcome Henry, Chris, Tyson, and especially Alexis into our family. Chris and Alexis have been really wonderful in having Dawn included in all of the wedding plans.

In many of these toasts, the best man talks about experiences with the groom. What can I say after twenty-eight years of so many great memories? I am so proud of all three of my sons in different ways, but Jason is special because he was number one, and I have known him longer.

Unforgettable times:

- *Day born*
- *Evil Kneivel—age six*
- *Altar boy*
- *St. Louis Christmas Plays*
- *Four years at Mt. St. Joe*
- *Skiing off mountain on a Mt. St. Joe ski trip*
- *Four years at University of Delaware*
- *Playing Division I lacrosse*
- *The evening he left for Telluride*
- *The day he returned from Telluride*
- *Career decision to work for family business*
- *The day he met Alexis*
- *The day he told us he was asking Alexis to marry him*
- *The evening he asked Alexis at a Ravens' game*
- *This wonderful wedding*

Spending a lot of time with Jason and his friends over the last couple of months reminds me of many good times watching all of these guys playing football and lacrosse, baseball and basketball, skiing and snowmobiling in Telluride, fishing trips to the Bay and the rivers out west. We are truly blessed with so many fond memories of Jason, his brothers, and his friends.

Alexis—as soon as we met you and saw you and Jason together, Dawn and I knew you were the one. You two look so good together and truly make each other happy. As you both go through your life together, always love one another, treat each other with respect, and continue to make each other happy.

And now the toast—may our good Lord always guide you and bless you, grant you many happy and healthy years together, give you many beautiful and healthy children, and always keep you both as happy as you are today.

Blase was certainly happy that night. In fact, in November, 2000, life was really going well for Blase and his family. His oldest son had just married a beautiful young lady and was working hard and doing well at Harkins Builders. Brian and Kevin, who were living in Oregon, were home for the wedding and an extended visit with Mom and Dad. Everything, as Blase would always say, was terrific!

Unfortunately, what no one knew at the time was that Blase's red face, which had been previously diagnosed as a minor skin disease called rosacea, was actually a symptom for carcinoid cancer. It was very probable that Blase had a cancerous tumor growing on his lung at that time. The symptoms you get with a carcinoid tumor will depend on what chemicals your tumor secretes into your bloodstream. One of the most common symptoms is skin flushing, where the skin on your face changes color—ranging from pink to red to purple. Blase definitely had that symptom, and over the next few months, developed another symptom of carcinoid: asthma-like wheezing and shortness of breath. No one really knows how long the cancer had been festering in his body.

**The happy best man and dad at
Jason's wedding**

***

Jason has wonderful memories of his childhood, probably because he was the only child for the first four years of his life and received all the attention. His very early memories were playing street ball and going on job sites with his dad. They would walk the job sites, and Jason would climb and play on the large construction equipment. He also remembers Blase coming home from work and announcing his arrival with a loud whistle. Jason would jump into his arms for a big hug and then sit down for a family dinner.

The family moved into their newly built home in Woodmark when Jason was about four and a half years old, at about the same time Brian was born. Much later in life, Blase told his sons that the closest he ever came to having a nervous breakdown was the timeframe when he purchased the lot for the new home, went through the process of building the home as the general contractor, worked his full-time job at Harkins, and then found out Dawn was pregnant with Kevin—all in a three-to-four-month period.

In the early days, most of Jason's memories revolved around sports. One of the first lessons he learned from his dad was how important it was to practice. He remembers many occasions when he and Blase would hit golf balls in the back yard to improve their short game or go to the Font Hill Driving Range to hit balls and play the par three course. All three of the boys played their first round of golf with their dad at Font Hill.

Blase started coaching basketball in the Howard County Youth Program (HCYP) when Jason was six years old; coached him until he was twelve, then circled back to coach Brian and Kevin. Jason remembered that Blase always seemed to draft the kids the other coaches didn't want. When Jason would ask why he picked a particular youngster who fell into that category, his response would always be that he thought he might be able to help that kid become a better player or person. When he wasn't coaching, he was almost always there watching and supporting his kids. In those rare instances where he couldn't make an event, he would make up for it by asking his sons to replay every minute of the game.

Blase was perhaps one of the most competitive people I have ever known, and I am certainly not alone in this observation. His boys grew up watching, admiring, and emulating his competitive spirit. In those days when he wasn't working and coaching, he was competing in all kinds of sports, including golf, of course, but also basketball, tennis, racquetball, softball, volleyball, pool, and table tennis. Everything was a competition. He even competed in Mrs. Pacman and Atari Pong tournaments. For those of you who don't remember, the Atari Pong game was the very first consumer-based video game. He also created or helped create events like the Brothers' Tennis Tournament (you had to have a brother to be in the tournament), and the SuperStars Competition (ten events played in one day). We even had a trophy made, and the winner would keep the trophy until the following year when the next winner was crowned.

Jason attended Mt. St. Joseph High School, which was a start to fulfilling one of Blase's lifetime goals—to send his children to the high school he was unable to attend. Jason played football and lacrosse at the varsity level. Blase had read somewhere that playing football at an early age could result in physical problems later on in life, so he would not permit his boys to play football until high school. Jason also enjoyed fishing and snow skiing, and joined St. Joe's ski club, where he would participate with his buddies in one or two ski trips per season.

Although Blase never grew up participating in any of these sports, he attempted to immerse himself into all of them at some level because of his desire to actively participate with his kids. In the case of lacrosse and football, his physical participation was limited to an occasional game of catch, but his real interest was being a fan and watching his sons compete. As soon as the game schedules were published, he would mark them in his calendar with the intent of getting to every game he possibly could. In other words, unlike most of us, he tried to work his family schedule around his business schedule as opposed to the other way around.

When it came to fishing and skiing, Blase took a much more active role. All three of the kids liked to fish, and they have very fond memories of fishing with their dad in the early evenings at a small lake near their home. As time went on, their excursions evolved into some deep-sea fishing and also included a week-long, guys-only fishing vacation and expedition to Alaska with one of Blase's best friends, Dave Carney, and his sons. When it came to skiing, however, Blase was challenged to keep up with his boys on the ski slopes. Let's just say that Blase really enjoyed "cruising" on the beginner slopes while his sons focused more on skiing and snowboarding on the black diamonds. A typical day would start with one or two family runs on a beginner slope, and then they would set a place and time to meet and eat somewhere on the mountain. This would be followed by another "green" run on a beginner slope, then a new plan to meet later in the day.

Blase and his boys in Colorado, 1992

Unlike some dads, Blase never pressured his boys to participate in a particular sport just because he may have liked it. Rather, he encouraged them to explore and seek out activities that they were interested in, and they did. He would then attempt to follow in their footsteps.

When it came to choosing a college, Blase gave Jason a tremendous amount of flexibility. He could go to any college he wanted, provided it was less than a three-and-a half hour trip by car. There were only two exceptions: Notre Dame, because Blase was Irish and Catholic and grew up dreaming of going to Notre Dame; and Clemson, because it was one of the only schools in the country that offered a construction management program. Jason had spent one summer during high school working at Harkins, and Blase, like any dad, would have loved to have one or more of his sons follow in his footsteps, but he never pushed it. According to Jason, this restriction on selecting a college was the most significant stipulation Jason ever received from his dad. Jason would have loved to go to school in Colorado because he was really hooked on skiing, but that was not to be.

In his senior year at St. Joe, Jason was approached by the lacrosse coach from the University of Delaware, who expressed an interest in having him play there. Since it met his dad's criteria, and since he still enjoyed playing lacrosse, he decided to go there.

Over the next couple of years, the family took some ski trips to Colorado, and Jason really got the bug. He struck a deal with his dad that if he graduated from college in four years, then Dad would assist him financially in getting set up out west. After graduating from Delaware on time, Jason ended up finding a job and living in Telluride for the next two years. He was loving life. The family spent their next two Christmas vacations in Telluride. In October, 1996, at twenty-four years old, Jason decided to come back home to Baltimore and he began working for Harkins Builders in the field as an assistant site manager on a very large building project in downtown Baltimore. Jason's biggest concern about working for Harkins was the fact that he was the boss's son. By working in the field, he was able to become his own person and establish his own identity. The project, which, at the time, was the largest project in Harkin's history, came in sixteen months ahead of schedule and was a huge success for the company.

Jason first met Alexis in Dewey Beach, Delaware in the summer of 1997. A couple of buddies suggested he invest in renting a small house for the summer with a bunch of other people. Jason thought it sounded like a good deal, and the price was right, so he opted in. He failed to ask a few key questions, like how many people had invested in this small house that comfortably sleeps eight people? The answer was twenty-two—ten ladies and twelve guys. His first visit to the beach house was the Fourth of July weekend. He drove down with a couple of buddies and they arrived late on Thursday evening around midnight. They were tired after a long day, so they decided to just hang out and have a couple of beers. At about 1:30 a.m., Jason saw a very attractive young lady come into the house with three girlfriends. Her name was Alexis, and her roommate had invited her down for the weekend. Jason was immediately attracted to her. The next day, a large group went out for lunch and Jason went out of his way to let Alexis know he was interested in her. Two weeks later, they were both back in Dewey Beach and they got to know each other better. Alexis found out Jason was nicknamed "Greg Brady" because of his long, curly hair, and Jason found out Alexis had a birthday coming up the following week on July 27. He called her that day to wish her a happy birthday and to ask her out on their first date. Alexis accepted, and from that point on, they were inseparable.

Soon after they met, Jason arranged for Alexis to meet Blase and Dawn. They had a wonderful dinner at the Inner Harbor in Baltimore. They both immediately realized Jason and Alexis would more than likely end up getting married. They were right because two years later, on November 4, 1999, Jason proposed to Alexis. It was at a Baltimore Ravens football game against the Kansas City Chiefs. The Ravens lost that night, but Jason won. Jason is an avid Ravens fan and thought this would be the perfect place to pop the question. Unlike the Ravens, he had developed a great game plan. He had four tickets located in the same section as the sky boxes at Ravens Stadium. Jason invited Alexis's best friend and her boyfriend to attend the game with them. With Blase's help, they arranged to have the engagement party in Bill Franey's sky box, which was located just to the right of the section where they were sitting. He had made an "Alexis, will you marry me?" sign which would be draped over the side of the sky box. The plan was to put the sign out at the end of the first quarter. Then Jason was going to take Alexis up toward the skybox to meet a fictitious friend, thus enabling her to see the sign. The skybox was filled with family and friends. As soon as Alexis noticed the sign and comprehended what was happening, Jason dropped to his knees, right in the middle of a bunch of Ravens fans, and proposed to her. It turned out to be a perfect evening, except of course, for the Ravens' loss.

***

It was May 10, 2003, at the Greater Baltimore Medical Center in Towson, Maryland. Dawn absolutely knew it was going to be a boy. Blase knew, like all other children born into this world, he was about to experience the miracle of birth, but this would be a very special miracle because it would be their first grandchild. Cecilia Kirsten Cooke was born, and needless to say, the parents and grandparents were ecstatic. She was a beautiful and healthy baby. Little Cecilia, or Cece as she is called, would develop a very special attachment to her poppy.

At the time Cece was born, Blase was two years into his cancer ordeal. Over the next couple of years, he had more terrific days than not-so-terrific days, enabling him to experience the joy of being a normal grandfather, taking her for walks, playing in the park, etc., and he relished the role of Poppy. Whenever he saw Cece, it immediately became a terrific day, no matter how he was feeling.

Alexis and Jason were blessed with their second child, Reeves, on August 19, 2005. He was named after one of Jason's best friends, Kevin Reeves, who died tragically in an avalanche in Telluride in 1997 at the young age of twenty-five. Reeves Joseph Cooke would be the firstborn male of the next generation to carry on the Cooke family name. By the time Reeves had learned to walk, Blase no longer could, but he loved holding Reeves, reading books to him, and riding him around in his wheelchair.

DeeDee and Poppy with Reeves and Cece

They say the apple doesn't fall too far from the tree, and in the case of Blase's sons, that is so true. Jason learned well from his dad. He was grateful for having a role model and a friend who was always there for him, and a person who had his priorities in order. In return, he made sure he was there to help Blase in his time of need. He told me he was fortunate to be in a position to get involved during Blase's illness. Harkins allowed Jason the flexibility to arrange his work schedule in order to help both Blase and Dawn get to doctors' appointments, hospital visits, lab tests, chemotherapy treatments, physical therapy, etc. For the last few years of Blase's illness, the vacation for Jason and his family was to visit Blase and Dawn for a week during the winter in Florida. Alexis and the kids loved the warm weather and the pool, and it was great to have Dawn and Aunt Joey, Dawn's sister, attending to the kids. Jason enjoyed just being there with his dad and helping him in any way he could.

The last vacation in Florida occurred in March, 2007. Blase had been doing some intense chemotherapy, and it was taking its toll on him. By the time Jason and the family arrived, Blase was very weak, so much so that on Sunday, March 11, 2007, he was admitted to the Southwest Regional Medical Center (SWRMC) in Fort Myers. He was diagnosed with dehydration and they immediately began treatment. Over the next couple of days, further tests discovered some bronchial issues, and the doctors recommended he have a bronchoscopy procedure. He had already had three previous bronchoscopies and wanted to consult with his doctors in Baltimore before agreeing to the procedure.

Like most people, Blase did not like hospitals. In fact, he absolutely hated them. As soon as he was admitted, the first thing he would do was figure out the quickest and most expedient way of getting out. In this particular case, the doctors at SWRMC felt strongly that he needed to have this procedure, and after checking with his Baltimore doctors, it was agreed it needed to be done.

Meanwhile, during a conversation with Jason, Blase mentioned he had received an insurance policy many years ago from one of his investment friends, which included a rider to cover an airlift from one hospital to another. This was typically used for people who may become ill or would get into an accident while traveling in another country and would want to be treated in the United States. Jason asked Blase if he had any information so he could do some research, and remarkably, Blase had the card in his wallet with the 800 number.

Jason immediately called to inquire if Blase qualified for an airlift. Not only did they answer yes, they quickly offered to make all the necessary arrangements. Because this was not considered a medical emergency, his policy did not cover airlifts on weekends. However, the medically-equipped private jet and medical staff could airlift Blase back to Baltimore on the following Monday.

Since Blase was scheduled to go back to Baltimore in April anyway, Jason thought this would make much more sense, especially given the difficulty Blase had flying down to Florida. It was the first time Blase had flown in an airplane since he had become a paraplegic, and it was very difficult, to say the least. However, there was one problem. It was Friday morning, March 16, and the hospital had just informed Blase the bronchoscopy procedure was scheduled for Monday, March 19.

Jason had a better idea. He immediately told Blase he had made the arrangements for the airlift team to pick him up on Monday, March 19, and they would airlift him to Howard County General Hospital. Jason had also decided he would work with the SWRMC hospital staff to try and reschedule the bronchoscopy procedure to Saturday or Sunday. Blase liked the idea. Of course, the hospital said it would be impossible to reschedule the procedure. Jason, in a polite, but firm way, responded that the airlift was already scheduled to transfer Blase to Baltimore, so he would not be available for the procedure on Monday. After asking a few questions, he was informed the real problem was the doctor scheduled to perform the procedure was not working that weekend. So Jason called the doctor, explained the situation, and the doctor was kind enough to perform a successful procedure on Saturday. Around midnight on Monday, March, 19, 2007, Blase arrived at Howard County General and would remain there for five more days recovering from the aftereffects from his chemotherapy treatment and dehydration.

Blase was very proud of what his son did for him. Although he remained in the hospital for five days after returning home to Baltimore, it was different. Blase was back in familiar surroundings, and at least for a while, he was off the chemo. He enjoyed telling family and friends the story surrounding the events, how well the medical team took care of him throughout the journey, and how his son helped him through a very difficult time.

There is no doubt in my mind how proud Blase must have felt when his spirit heard the beautiful tribute Jason made to his dad, his best man.

Phil Cooke

Excerpt from Jason's Eulogy to Blase—October 5, 2007

*It is a sad occurrence of life that brings us here today, but it is
also a great man that brings us all here together. A man that
does not want us to mourn the passing of his time here on
Earth, but rather, a man that wants us to celebrate the times we
have shared with him and carry on the lessons he has taught us.*

*Blase's long battle with cancer has allowed us to prepare for
this moment, but nothing can fully prepare you for the void that
is left with him no longer here. I ask that we all try to fill this
void by honoring Blase by living each day with the same
passion, faith, and enthusiasm that he did, staying together as
one large family, helping others in need, volunteering our time
and money, raising our children with lots of love and attention,
and remembering the good times. There were so many.*

So many thoughts and memories come rushing into my head . . .

*playing stick ball with him in Medwick Garth, going to
construction sites on Saturdays, building our house in
Woodmark, seeing him on the sidelines at our sporting events,
watching him compete in softball, racquetball, cards and golf,
having dinner together every evening at seven, going to
church with him on Sundays, learning to play golf from him,
playing in his favorite foursome . . . Dad and his three boys. I
also know how much he enjoyed playing with so many of you,
our times at the beach with the best of friends, the parties, all
the Christmases and holidays, so many trips... skiing at Wisp
and out west (where he broke his leg on a run called Synch,
but told anyone who asked he did it doing a helicopter off of
Belly Grabbers' Ditch, our male bonding trip to Alaska,
seeing him dance in a ring of fire in Greece and seeing him*

My Brother, My Keeper

*dance again when he placed a live octopus in his bathing suit,
going to work for him at Harkins Builders . . . how proud I
was of him as he motivated everyone towards a common goal
that the company was going to achieve in the upcoming year,
and how he would ask anyone to ask any questions that they
had—and he would stand there in silence until somebody
asked at least one question.*

*His best man speech at my wedding, that look in his eye when I
told him we were pregnant, the look on his face when he held
his grandchildren or when one of them called him Poppy and
the way he would look at Mom.*

*There are so many of you that could be up here paying tribute
to my dad . . . Joseph Peter Blase Cooke. This fact is a tribute
to him and shows how many people he has touched, how many
problems he has helped solve, and how many friends he has. We
want to thank you for your prayers and support.*

Some things that I will never forget about my dad:

*He was a great son, brother, friend, leader, husband, dad, and
poppy.*

*He was an incredible leader of so many things: Harkins
Builders, Catholic Charities, government boards, and especially
our family.*

*He always had time for those that needed him or just a needed
some reassurance or a kind word.*

*Hearing others ask him how he was doing . . . and hearing
"TERRIFIC."*

Phil Cooke

I will never forget the fight he showed during this battle with cancer and the will he showed to live another day . . . to quote Jimmy Valvano, "Cancer can take away all of my physical abilities. It cannot touch my mind, it cannot touch my heart, and it cannot touch my soul. And these three things are going to carry on forever. . . . Don't give up, don't ever give up" Dad, we all know you never gave up! Rest in peace.

Memorandum

To: Thought For The Day Recipients

From: Blase Cooke

Re: **THE TEN COMMANDMENTS OF GETTING ALONG WITH PEOPLE**

---

1. *Keep skid chains on your tongue. Always say less than you think. Cultivate a low, persuasive voice. How you say it often counts more than what you say.*
2. *Make promises sparingly and keep them faithfully.*
3. *Never let an opportunity pass to say a kind and encouraging word to or about somebody. Praise good work.*
4. *Be interested in others: their pursuits, their work, their homes, and their families. Be sincere in your interest.*
5. *Be cheerful. Don't burden those around you by dwelling on your aches and pains and disappointments. Remember, people have troubles of their own.*
6. *Keep an open mind. Discuss, but don't argue. A mark of greatness is to be able to disagree without becoming disagreeable.*
7. *Let your virtues speak for themselves. Refuse to talk about the vices of others. Discourage gossip.*
8. *Take into consideration the feelings of others. Wit and humor at the expense of others are never worth the pain inflicted.*
9. *Pay no attention to ill-mannered remarks about you. Remember, they cast doubt on the character of the speaker, not on yours.*
10. *Don't be anxious about receiving the credit due to you. Do your best and be patient. Your reward will surely come.*

Chapter 7

Cancer Detected—Mother's Day, May 11, 2001

"The lesson that Blase taught me personally as a neurologist was to reinforce the importance of hope and optimism."

Dr. Justin McArthur, December 12, 2007

In the spring of 2001, Blase was having some minor issues with constant wheezing and coughing, as well as occasional pains in his chest, so he went to his doctor to have it checked. You need to understand that, beginning in his early twenties, Blase had became a poster boy for eating well and staying in top shape both physically and mentally. In his younger days, he felt invincible, so he didn't worry much about his health, and like most of us at that age, he took it for granted. He had always been in good physical shape. He played lots of sports and liked to work out and lift weights. His early days in construction were physically demanding as well, but in those days, he smoked cigarettes, consumed alcohol, ate whatever he wanted and didn't worry too much about the consequences. As he grew older and matured, got married and began to have children, he realized he was responsible for much more than just himself. He also knew his dad was a smoker, liked his Manhattans, and he didn't take time to exercise. In the fifties, most people probably had similar habits because they didn't fully understand the potential negative consequences to a person's health like we do today, not to mention, when your father drops dead from a massive heart attack, it has a lasting impression on your own mortality.

As soon as Blase began to carry the responsibility of a wife and children, he decided he was going to take care of himself in order to make every effort to avoid the fate of his father. In his early twenties, he stopped smoking completely, continued to exercise, and developed a healthy diet. His alcohol consumption reverted to an occasional glass of wine or a beer. He also liked what we affectionately referred to as "girly drinks," strawberry daiquiris, piña coladas, etc., and would occasionally have one. He justified those types of drinks because of the "healthy" fruit content. He carried these healthy habits throughout the rest of his adult life. He went from chocolate donuts to bran muffins, from whiskey sours to orange juice, and from hamburgers to turkey burgers. If he did have a vice, it was his love for sweets, especially ice cream, but he consumed those treats in moderation—most of the time.

Some might say he went to extremes in his quest to live to a ripe old age. He would read or hear about some new health fad, do the research, and if he thought it made sense, he would take action. I'll give you two examples. The first is blue-green algae, a nutritional supplement. According to the Wellness Center at the University of California, blue-green algae is an important part of the food chain in lakes and ponds worldwide. They are microscopic plants with characteristics of both bacteria and algae (such as seaweed), but are more closely akin to bacteria. Blue-green algae contain small amounts of protein, vitamins (including C, E, and foliate), beta carotene, and some minerals, but unless you eat huge amounts of algae, they are a negligible source of nutrients. Blase took blue-green algae pills on a daily basis for most of his adult life. One of the first things that came to my mind when I found out he had cancer was that damn algae. Could the algae have actually caused the cancer? Ironically, some of the purported benefits supposedly include prevention of cancer and heart disease. Given the family history of heart disease, perhaps he thought it might help to prevent it. The UC Berkley report goes on to say that blue-green algae is not a medicine or a good source of nutrients. The few nutrients in blue-green algae are more plentiful and cheaper in the food we eat. There's no scientific evidence that blue-green algae can treat or cure any illness or has any health benefit.

Blase was also a big believer in magnet therapy. Practitioners claim that subjecting certain parts of the body to magneto static fields has beneficial health effects, including the treatment of arthritis, wrist, and back pain. It has been used historically in many different civilizations as a natural healing technique. Blase wore a magnetic bracelet, which is used by many golfers to address various aches and pains. He also had a magnetic mattress, which he hoped would help him with his chronic back problems. He believed in magnet therapy so much that he sometimes shared it with friends like Rocco, as mentioned earlier. The point to be made here is that Blase wanted to live a long and healthy life, and he worked hard at it. He was very proactive in doing everything he could in body and mind to live every day in a healthy way in order to live as long as he could.

On Mother's Day weekend, 2001, most of our family traveled to Ocean City, Maryland to celebrate the christening of our niece, Ellen Marie. A few days before the event, Blase had an x-ray and it revealed a mass on his left lung. Further tests were scheduled. The morning of the christening, Blase decided to tell Dawn there would be more tests, but told her not to worry because he was sure it would not be serious. I suspect, at some level, he sensed he might have a potentially serious health issue, but he refused to allow that thought to enter his conscious mind. He was not going to let a potentially "temporary inconvenience," as he would later call it, get him down or negatively impact his positive outlook on life.

Over the next few weeks, Blase went through a series of tests, and unfortunately, the results were not good. In fact, the news was horrible. The tests had revealed a large tumor on his lung and the biopsy confirmed he had carcinoid cancer. When Blase received the test results in the last week of June, Dawn was in Bermuda on a short vacation with Sister Lois, a friend of Dawn's. As soon as he mentioned that the doctor wanted to see both of them together, she immediately knew it was bad news. The official meeting with Blase, Dawn, and his doctor took place on July 2, 2001. Life as they knew it would be drastically changed forever.

The meeting with Dr. Oden was surreal. He explained that the test results showed a tumor on the lung and two small spots on his liver which required further tests. It was a rare form of cancer called carcinoid cancer. Carcinoid cancers are typically small, slow-growing tumors found mostly in the gastrointestinal system, but can be in other parts of the body such as the stomach, lung, and liver. Since most of these tumors grow very slowly compared to other cancers, it usually takes many years before they become sizable or cause symptoms. Since no one could determine how long Blase's cancer had been there, they could not determine how fast it had grown. What they did know was that the tumor on his lung was abnormally large.

The doctor helped them set up their next meeting with an oncologist. By this point, they were both numb. They heard what was said, but it was extremely difficult to process what they had just heard. They walked out of the doctor's office and as soon as they got to the car, they both cried for what seemed to be a very long time. After the crying subsided, Dawn told Blase that they would get through this together and she would be there for him. The very next day, they began the process of developing a plan to win this battle. One of the most difficult challenges they faced immediately was delivering the news to their children. Of course, Blase delivered this message in a very positive and uplifting manner, telling the kids that life would go on as usual, they would handle this challenge together, and everything would turn out fine.

During their first meeting with the oncologist, they learned the follow-up testing on his liver revealed cancerous tumors, and he would need surgery on his liver as well. The reality of the situation was incredibly frightening. Had the cancer metastasized? To be honest, after consulting with other doctors, we learned later that, depending on what doctor you talked to, you would get a different answer. No one really knew for sure, but what was really amazing was that Blase did not look at this situation and say, "Why me, Lord?" He did not dwell on the fact that he might die. He took a positive approach. He was somehow going to figure out how to turn this lemon into lemonade, but this challenge would, without question, become the biggest he would ever face in his life.

One of Blase's first and certainly not last suggestions to his doctors was to knock out both surgeries at the same time, sort of a two for one deal. He wanted to avoid going through two recovery periods. Not only was he thinking about ridding himself from cancer, he wanted to do so as quickly as possible.

On September 12, 2001, four months after the initial tests revealed the mass on his lung, and the day after the World Trade Center tragedy, Blase had the cancerous tumor, as well as approximately one-third of the lower lobe of his left lung, removed. The surgeon had to remove one of his ribs before he could extract the tumor. Somehow, all of Blase's annual physicals never identified this intrusive growth on his lung. Immediately after the operation, the surgeon believed he had "gotten everything" and deemed the surgery a "success." We thanked God for answering our prayers.

For more than six years, he would endure daily medications and needles, untold numbers of doctors' appointments, blood tests, MRIs, CT scans, surgeries, radiation, chemotherapy, and numerous hospital stays. And to be perfectly blunt, in the entire time of his ordeal, there was hardly ever any good news, unless of course you looked at things the way Blase did—always striving to find something positive. He needed to find something positive because he didn't want to have to tell his kids he was dying. Ultimately, the cancer would also take away his ability to walk as it eventually crept into his spine, making him a paraplegic.

Phil Cooke

From Dawn's perspective, of all the challenges Blase faced throughout his ordeal with cancer, his paralysis was the most difficult for him. And it was for her as well. She could no longer cuddle up with him because the parts of his body that he did feel became extremely sensitive, even painful to the touch. For the last eighteen months of the ordeal, he was in constant pain. The most difficult times for them both were the long nights when it was just the two of them alone. Blase's hospital bed became a metal cage which separated them from being able to hold each other. Losing the physical contact was most difficult for Dawn because she wanted and needed to cling to him and Blase was unable to do so. Practically every night, Blase would wake up in pain, unable to move, and needing to be turned to more comfortable position. He hated to have to wake up Dawn so he would lie there awake, hoping she would stir. But Dawn was always there to help him. These were clearly the darkest and most difficult times for both of them, and the saddest. But somehow, the next morning, they would get out of bed to start a new day. And somehow, they were both able to leave the anger, frustration, sadness, and most of the tears in the bedroom.

Thank God for Dawn's baby sister, Joelyn, our angel from Las Vegas. Joey was very grateful to Dawn and Blase because they had always been there for her. The first thing Joey said to Dawn when she was told of Blase's cancer was that she would be there for them whenever they needed her. Whenever they talked on the phone, Joey would always remind Dawn that she was ready to come to Baltimore to help care for Blase. She had seen Blase and Dawn over the next few years when she would come back for visits and they were handling things quite well. In September, 2005 Joey came back to Baltimore for the groundbreaking ceremony, and she saw major changes in Blase since she had last seen him at the My Brother's Keeper dinner in April. Although he still seemed mentally sound, he was certainly not the Blase she knew. He had become very frail and was having serious difficulty walking. Over the coming months, Joey constantly reiterated her offer to help. In May 2006, Joey moved into their home and became Blase's full-time caregiver (and angel from God).

116

Needless to say, she also became a source of support and inspiration to Dawn as well.

When Joey left Las Vegas, she had a sense she would probably not return. Her daughter, Dana, and her two grandchildren were already living in Maryland. Her son, Anthony, stayed in Las Vegas and moved back into his mom's condominium. This was a significant lifestyle change for Joey. She had lived in Vegas for thirteen years, and had been divorced and living independently for four years. But she was ready to take on this new challenge.

When Joey arrived, Blase had just endured major back surgery and he was in rehabilitation, with a strong desire to walk again in time for his son, Kevin's, wedding in June. Joey, who was into physical fitness herself, was looking forward to helping Blase reach his goal to walk again. Dawn, on the other hand, had been through five demanding years of watching Blase endure so much. Joey's positive outlook and her eagerness to help both Dawn and Blase was a very positive shot in the arm for everyone, and they were able to inspire each other to keep on going. Joey was clearly a blessing from God. Taking care of Blase was a "labor of love" for Joey. Her love for Blase and how he handled the illness day in and day out was what inspired her to do what she did every day for the next eighteen months until he died. And never did Blase ever refuse to do his "daily workout" with Joey.

***

What follows is a chronology of the major events regarding Blase's history with cancer. Interestingly, in the fifty-four years prior to getting cancer, Blase was in the hospital only three times: an appendectomy at age seven, a tonsillectomy at age eleven, and a hernia at age forty-three. Until the cancer struck, he had been a very healthy man.

Interspersed throughout this chronology are "updates" from Blase on his condition and his unyielding positive state of mind over the course of his cancer journey. Blase had received literally hundreds of cards, notes, and emails from family, friends, and business associates, among others, and he found the most effective way he could keep up would be to send out an occasional email describing his progress. I think you will find these notes both interesting and inspiring.

Cancer Chronology

July 2, 2001	Cancer diagnosed
September 12, 2001	Surgery to remove lower lobe of left lung (ten days)
January 31, 2002	Liver surgery—70% of liver removed (ten days)
March, 2002	First meeting with Dr. Larry Kvols, carcinoid expert, Moffet Research Center, Tampa, Florida
July 11, 2002	First meeting with Dr. Pommier, carcinoid expert, Portland, Oregon
September, 2002	First chemoembolization procedure on liver
March 11, 2003	First round of chemotherapy
July 29, 2003	First bronchoscopy
August 25, 2003	First round of radiation—three weeks
November 11, 2003	Second bronchoscopy
December, 2003	Second round of chemotherapy
February, 2004	Third round of chemotherapy
May 4, 2004	Third bronchoscopy
November, 2004	Second round of radiation
December, 2004	Fourth round of chemotherapy—Zometa—intravenous chemotherapy every three weeks through February, 2005

May, 2005	Fifth round of chemotherapy—Avastin— intravenous chemotherapy every three weeks through July, 2005
May 12, 2006	Spinal surgery at Johns Hopkins Hospital (six days)

Dr. Justin McArthur, a noted neurosurgeon from Johns Hopkins University Hospital, met Blase in the spring of 2006 when Blase was having tremendous difficulty walking. He could immediately discern how determined Blase was to walk again, and he suggested back surgery in an attempt to help him reach this goal. The doctors could not determine if his paralysis had been caused by his chronic back problems he had endured over many years or the tumors which had spread into his bone and were extremely close to his spinal cord. There was also the concern that his radiation treatments could have potentially caused the paralysis. Unfortunately, the surgery was not successful.

Like Blase, Dr. McArthur refused to give up, and he recommended Blase be tested to enter a specialized program at the world-renowned Kennedy Krieger Institute's International Center for Spinal Cord Injury, where they perform leading-edge research using activity-based therapy to treat spinal cord injuries. Blase was accepted into the home-based portion of the program and immediately incorporated a new exercise program into his daily schedule. He had a special bike that used a motor to get him started and then electrical stimulation that prompted his major muscle groups to the point where he could actually use his own muscles to propel the bike, even though he couldn't feel anything or move the pedals on his own. There was a computer on the bike which was networked into Kennedy Krieger, where they monitored the program and kept records of each session and his progression. Blase worked diligently on his bike exercise on a daily basis for seven months, but to no avail. Dr. McArthur would come to visit Blase at his home occasionally to see how he was doing. What he learned from these visits was that Blase did not want to give up.

Below is a letter from Dr. McArthur which illustrates the importance and value of maintaining a positive attitude and always striving to overcome obstacles.

December 12, 2007

Dear Mr. Cooke,

Over twenty years of practice, I have been honored to participate in the care of thousands of patients, and I have strong memories of many of them. Few come close to having the kind of impact on my practice as a physician as Blase did. From our first meeting, it was, unfortunately, all too clear that he had serious neurological problems, which we might not be able to reverse. Despite my less-than-rosy prognosis, Blase immediately leapt at the possibility of reversal and recovery, and I think what struck me so definitively was his drive, relentless optimism, and ability to overcome, or at least to attempt to overcome, both physical and mental challenges. Within the first few weeks of our medical journey together, it became clear that his walking would not return. Even this news did not deter him from researching the subject online, talking to other physicians, and challenging me to research other alternative therapies. Blase was in charge, not me, and he made that very clear in his own firm, yet polite way over the subsequent months. There were many times when Blase's spirits sagged, understandably, but he refused to give in to his disease and was seeking solutions and exploring new strategies up until the end.

The lesson that Blase taught me personally as a neurologist was to reinforce the importance of hope and optimism. I have always strived to find some treatment, some strategy, and some intervention which can be done. Blase emphasized to me in many ways that the words "never" and "cannot" should not be in a physician's vocabulary. For that reason, he has made an indelible impression on me.

Yours sincerely,

Justin C. McArthur, M.B.B.S., M.P.H
Professor, Departments of Neurology, Pathology, and Epidemiology
Interim Chair, Department of Neurology

***

Cancer Chronology *(cont.)*

May 23, 2006   Rehab at Good Samaritan Hospital (two weeks)
July 7, 2006   Blood infusion at Howard County Hospital
July 20, 2006   Admitted to Johns Hopkins due to paralysis problems
Diagnosed as a paraplegic (four weeks, including occupational therapy)

Email from Blase dated Friday, August 11, 2006

Hi All –

Hope everyone is doing well. I have some good news and bad news!

The bad news is they are keeping me in rehab for an extra week. My discharge date is now August 22, which has been pushed back from August 15.

The good news is that we are making some progress. I am getting some feelings back below my waist and I am getting a little bit of my strength back. I continue to work hard and I am starting to get my mind set and attitude adjusted to continue this difficult journey to walk again.

Once again, thanks to all of you for your thoughts, prayers, cards, and e-mails. I'm sorry I'm not able to respond personally.

Be well,

Blase

Despite his diagnosis as a paraplegic, Blase still refused to give up. He was inspired by two amazing success stories from the Kennedy Krieger Institute, Christopher Reeves and Pat Rummerfield, who both made miraculous progress. Pat, for example, is missing two-thirds of his spinal column due to a serious car crash many years ago, and today is considered the world's most fully functioning quadriplegic. He has competed in triathlons and is an accomplished race car driver in spite of the fact that he can't feel his arms and legs. It's clear from Blase's words below that he showed similar determination.

***

Email from Blase dated Monday, January 8, 2007

Hello, everyone,

It is said that every long journey starts with the first step. Every morning, I wake up and try to move my toes. Recently, I have seen some movement, which is a good sign. Even though I expect movement every morning, that's not the case quite yet.

*My next big journey starts tomorrow when we head to Florida
and get away from this balmy weather. I know I'll be happy
when I get there, but the anticipation of the trip has been
overwhelming. I know that God's healing includes fresh
air and sunshine, which will soon be unavailable to me
at home.*

*The challenge now is to get through the muscle spasms and
some different pains that come and go, and to try hard to get my
strength back. These are short-term goals. I will also be
spending some time at H. Lee Moffittt Cancer Center for
ongoing cancer treatment. As you all know, my long-term goals
are to walk again and be cancer-free.*

*The very best to everyone for a happy, healthy, and blessed
New Year.*

Be well,

Blase

***

Cancer Chronology *(cont.)*

February 23, 2007	Fifth round of chemotherapy (five months)
March 11, 2007	Southwest Regional Medical Center for dehydration
March 16, 2007	Fourth bronchoscopy
March 19, 2007	Airlifted to Howard County Hospital (five days)
August, 2007	Second chemoembolization procedure on liver

Phil Cooke

September 25, 2007   Howard County Hospital—dehydration

2001–2007   Ongoing issues resulting from surgery, chemotherapy, radiation, and paralysis

- Bowel and urinary
- Spasms
- Pins and needles
- Back and stomach pain
- Hyperesthesia
- Instability and weakness
- Generally tired

In looking back at his records over the time in which he suffered with cancer, we estimate Blase averaged approximately fifty visits a year to either a doctor's office or lab to be poked or prodded in one way or another. And to be perfectly honest, most, if not all of the medical reports and test results were not good. But somehow he tried to help all of us focus on the good news—some tumors reduced in size, no additional tumors, positive blood count indicators, slight movement in his toes. Perhaps it was his way of getting the rest of us through the ordeal.

Blase managed his cancer treatment in much the same way he managed his entire adult life. He was positive and proactive. He set goals and objectives and then implemented a plan to achieve those goals and objectives. He was a leader. He handled his cancer treatment just like he handled any other challenge he faced. He researched and found the best doctors possible to help him win this battle. He explored every potential alternative, literally to the end.

Family photo—January, 2004

Blase's last update follows.

Email from Blase dated Monday, July 2, 2007

Hello, everyone.

It's been six months (1/8/07) since I sent out the last update. I certainly didn't expect to be so long between updates. I've been waiting for some good news to share with everyone. Unfortunately, that's why the updates were so far apart.

I've been on chemotherapy for the past five months, which has added new problems and issues to my already weakened condition. The recent test results were not what we were expecting. We are increasing the dosage of chemo by 50% and eliminating one of the other chemo cocktails.

I'm having four to five decent days in a month, so it's hard to see people. Hopefully the new treatment will be better. Actually, they gave me the past week off—it was the best week I've had to see people and appreciate those that dropped by.

I'm hoping to be in touch soon with some good news. Even though it's difficult, I have not given up on my goals to walk again and stabilize the cancer. Thanks to everyone for your thoughts, prayers, cards, and e-mails. It is good to hear from you.

Sincerely,

Blase

Memorandum

To: All Personnel

From: Blase Cooke

Re: THOUGHT FOR THE DAY

Attitude

"The longer I live, the more I realize the impact of attitude on life. Attitude, to me, is more important than the past, than education, than money, than circumstances, than failures, than successes, than what other people think or say or do. It is more important than appearance, giftedness, or skill. It will make or break a company . . . a church . . . a home.

"The remarkable thing is we have a choice every day regarding the attitude we will embrace for that day. We cannot change our past. We cannot change the fact that people will act in a certain way. We cannot change the inevitable. The only thing we can do is play on the one string we have, and that is our attitude.

"I am convinced that life is ten percent what happens to me and ninety percent how I react to it. And so it is with you . . . we are in charge of our ATTITUDES!"

By Charles Swindoll

Thank you to my niece, Nicol Cooke (Pomeroy), for this Thought for the Day.

Chapter 8

Brian and Kerri's Wedding—
Mount Hood, Oregon, July 13, 2002

"My father was a simple man. He prayed, took care of his health, worked hard, and loved harder . . ."

Brian Cooke Eulogy—October 5, 2007

Mount Hood, Oregon was, without question, the perfect spot for Brian and Kerri's wedding celebration. How did they end up choosing a place almost three thousand miles away from where they both grew up? That's a good question. First and foremost, they absolutely love the outdoors. And in Brian's case, his love of the outdoors started with his earliest memories, hitting golf balls with cut-off clubs, riding his Big Wheel in the driveway, and playing T-ball with his baby brother, Kevin. In fact, since they were born only sixteen months apart, every childhood memory he has includes Kevin. They did everything together, including playing organized sports, with their dad never far away—either coaching or cheering them on.

When it came to Blase's work life at Harkins, Brian did not have as many memories as Jason. He does remember going to the office occasionally with his mom. He loved to look at all the pictures in his office. And he admits even today that he really wasn't very interested with what his dad did for a living. In fact, the most dominant single memory of Blase's work life was the folder. It was a constant in all their lives, but not Blase's priority.

What Brian really remembers and appreciates most in his formative years growing up was not Blase's job, or the big house with the swimming pool and tennis court, or the organized sports in which he participated, but rather, it was watching, enjoying, and participating with his parents, family, and friends in everyday activities. There always seemed to be parties, cookouts, reunions, and get-togethers, which would include activities like talking, dancing, joking around, competing, and just having fun. Brian was talking about observing the adults doing these things, and as he grew up and matured, he realized what he really saw were loving relationships, strong friendships, and true bonding among family and friends. Fortunately for our family, our children have carried on that tradition with their families, extended families, and friends.

Annual family/friends vacation trips to Ocean City, Maryland were also another favorite for Brian, including the three-hour drive to the beach itself. One of Brian's favorite memories was hearing his dad sing (and I use that term very loosely) his rendition of Neil Diamond's "Coming to America" while crossing the Chesapeake Bay Bridge. As Blase would approach the Bay Bridge toll plaza, he would play Neil Diamond's "Jazz Singer" as a prelude to the song he loved to sing while crossing the bridge. The Chesapeake Bay Bridge is a four-mile suspension bridge which crosses the Chesapeake Bay into Maryland's Eastern Shore. At its highest point, the bridge is 187 feet above the bay and pretty scary to some folks, like Blase. Much later in life, Brian was told the real reason Blase sang that Neil Diamond song was to help alleviate his anxiety regarding the height of the bridge.

Brian and Kevin also shared Jason's passion for skiing, which for them began while they were still in grade school. During the winter, they both played intramural basketball in the Howard County Youth Program. At that time, Blase and I were discussing the possibility of investing in a small ski house at the Wisp Ski Resort, located in the Allegheny Mountains in Western Maryland. At the foot of the mountain is Deep Creek Lake, which makes the area a four-season resort. When his children were much younger, Blase and the family had vacationed at Deep Creek Lake, and they loved the area. However, Blase felt in order to justify investing in the ski house, he needed to determine if Brian and Kevin would be willing to give up basketball, which would then free up their weekends for skiing. Brian still remembers Blase asking them what they wanted to do rather than telling them what he was going to do. The boys jumped at the opportunity to ski more often, thus ending their amateur basketball careers. Keep in mind that Blase was not a skier. In fact, he hated cold, snowy weather. However, he knew how much his boys loved skiing and he also realized these weekend ski trips with his family would result in lots of bonding and fond memories—he was right.

Along with Jason, Brian, and Kevin got their first taste of the big mountains out west when they went on a number of male bonding ski trips to Snowmass with the Carney family. They fell in love with that area of the country. In high school, they too joined the Mt. St. Joe ski club, and, like Jason, Brian played lacrosse. He fondly remembers how Blase would try to come to every game and would always discuss and analyze the whole experience. Win or lose, Blase would always find something positive to convey to Brian. Kevin was not much into contact sports, so he played on the St. Joe golf team. Win or lose, Blase always enjoyed watching his matches as well.

When it came time to send out college applications, Brian seemed bound and determined to attend the University of Colorado (and major in skiing). He had no desire to even apply anywhere else. This obviously did not meet the rule of going to a college within a three-and-a-half hour drive from home. Brian was aware of the stipulation, but he decided to push the envelope a bit. Blase was at least receptive to having him apply, but he made no promises. He and Dawn wanted Brian to apply to at least four other schools that met the guidelines, so Brian applied to four other colleges, two of which were Virginia Tech and the University of Delaware. He thought applying to Delaware would sit well with his parents since they were pleased with Jason's success and the fact that Jason set the family standard by completing his education within four years. He had heard Virginia Tech was a "cool school," so he applied there as well. As fate would have it, he was accepted to every school except the University of Colorado. The question is, was it fate, or were Blase's prayers answered?

To his parents' surprise, Brian chose Virginia Tech, but his stay there was short-lived. He had only been on campus a total of three days. When he returned to his dorm after his second day of classes, he found the local police in his room. The night before, he and his two roommates had watched a Monday night football game. They had consumed some beer and apparently smoked some marijuana, and the next morning, the campus police found remnants of the contraband from the night before. Brian and his friends were told by a campus advisor, if found guilty, they would eventually be suspended sometime in the current semester. Although he had only been in college for two days, he was smart enough to ask what was going to happen to him upon his return. He was told there would be a hearing in about three months, at which time he would probably be found guilty and formally suspended from school for the previous semester, and none of his coursework would be accredited.

Brian chose to contact his dad to seek his advice on how to handle the situation. And Blase responded. As it turned out, classes at the University of Delaware had not started yet, so Blase contacted the school and Brian was able to get into Delaware in time to start his first semester there.

At that point in his life, that phone call to his dad was the hardest thing he had ever done. He knew Blase would be very upset and extremely disappointed—and he was. His biggest disappointment was the fact that Brian had experimented with drugs. Blase had never tried marijuana, or any other illegal substance for that matter (unless blue algae is considered an illegal substance), and he was concerned it could potentially lead to Brian experimenting in other more serious drugs. Brian knew he had made a big mistake and had caused significant grief for his mom and dad. He expected he would probably end up either not going to college for a while or perhaps being told he would be going to a local community college. Rather, his dad was there to help him by suggesting he think about what he did, learn from his mistake, and move on. So a week after the incident at Virginia Tech, Brian was going to class at the University of Delaware and feeling very grateful his parents had accepted the fact that he had made a big mistake, but he also recognized and believed he had learned something from that experience.

It's funny how a single event in one's life can have such a dramatic impact on the rest of your life. Shortly after Brian arrived on the Delaware campus, he got involved in ultimate Frisbee. It became his passion. The object of the sport is to score points by passing a disc to a player in the opposing end zone, similar to an end zone in football or rugby. Players may not run while holding the disc. Ultimate is distinguished by its spirit of the game—the principles of fair play, sportsmanship, and the joy of play. In 1995, Brian started and was the captain of the first ultimate club team at the University of Delaware.

His love for ultimate actually led him to the ultimate love of his life, Kerri. There was both a male team and a coed team at Delaware. Brian was constantly looking for great male, and in particular, female players to add to the team. In the spring of 1997, a "hot new girl" showed up for practice. Kerri was not only a real cutie, but she had more raw talent than most of the girls who had already been playing for the past couple of years. Brian was definitely attracted to her, but it took him two months before he got the nerve to ask her out. In fact, he really didn't ask her out on a date. He found out she did not have any plans for her twenty-first birthday, so he offered to take her out to celebrate.

The first time Kerri met Blase and Dawn was when Brian brought her to a family wedding in October, 1997. A few weeks after the wedding,

Kerri and Brian made their first weekend visit to the family home in Woodmark. Kerri, who grew up in a rural area in Pennsylvania, was a bit overwhelmed when she saw the big house with the swimming pool and the tennis court. What really impressed her, however, was how comfortable she felt around Blase and Dawn. What she saw in Blase was a genuine person who had his priorities straight, and no ego. At dinner that evening, Dawn had prepared corn on the cob, which turned out to be a favorite of both Kerri and Blase. Kerri apparently loved corn even more than Blase and proceeded to eat six ears, including the last piece, and Blase never let her forget it.

Brian and Kerri dated steadily until graduating from Delaware in June, 1999. Since Brian was on a five-year college tour, and Kevin and Kerri were on the four-year plan, they all graduated at the same time. As a graduation present, Blase and Dawn had planned a trip to Rhodes, Greece to visit our cousin, Kathleen, who has lived with her husband, George, in the little town of Faliraki since their marriage in 1979. Kathleen was one of Aunt Rita's children, and over the years, many of our extended family have visited with Kathy, George, and their two boys, Dimitri and Visili. George and Kathy have owned and operated their little family run hotel/bar in this beautiful town on the Mediterranean Sea for more than twenty years. If you are ever looking for a wonderful and authentic Greek experience, look up George and Kathy at the Canon Bar in Faliraki. Believe me, you won't be disappointed. Since both Jason and Brian were in pretty serious relationships, Blase and Dawn asked if they were interested in Alexis and Kerri coming on the trip, and they jumped at the opportunity. Blase's only request was that the girls room together. They had a wonderful vacation.

After returning from Greece, Brian and Kerri decided to head to Oregon. They had considered California or Colorado as well, but they settled on Oregon because one of their former ultimate teammates had moved there and loved it, and given their mutual love for ultimate

Frisbee, snowboarding, and an outdoor lifestyle, it became an easy choice. Blase and Dawn would visit them in the spring or summer. Brian and Kerri would get back home for family events and visit a couple of times a year as well. On one trip to Oregon, knowing Brian's love for the outdoors, Blase surprised him by planning a fly fishing outing. He purchased a bunch of gear, took a training class in a field, and then they hit the river. Talk about a male bonding experience. . . . On another trip, they actually set out for the Upper Klamath Lake in southern Oregon, where much of the blue-green algae is harvested. Blase always seemed interested in whatever his boys were interested in. More than anything, he just loved being with them, being a dad.

About a year later, in the summer of 2000, Brian and Kerri had settled into a comfortable and happy lifestyle in Oregon. Kerri was finishing up some courses to become certified as a teacher, and Brian landed a teaching job for an elementary school nearby. Of course, they were enjoying all their treasured outdoor activities. While Kerri was starting to think more seriously about the future, Brian was trying to determine when and how he was going to pop the question. Thanks to his mom, he already had an engagement ring. Blase had given Dawn a piece of jewelry years ago which had three diamonds. Dawn had decided to give each of the boys a diamond, which could be made into an engagement ring. In October, 2000, Brian and Kerri were riding on an icy road not too far from their home in Ashland when Kerri lost control of the car and it flipped over. Fortunately, no one was hurt seriously. However, it made Brian realize how short life can be and how suddenly one incident can change your life forever. The following week, Brian drove Kerri out into the Oregon wilderness, stopped the car, and proposed to her.

Planning for the wedding began in the summer of 2001, which was right around the time Blase discovered he had cancer. Brian and Kerri immediately wanted to come back to Baltimore, but Blase was adamant. He told them not to change their lives, not to even think about it. Truth be told, Blase would have loved to have all his children, their spouses, and the grandchildren living close by so he could enjoy them as often as possible, but it wasn't about him. He certainly wasn't going to lure his loved ones closer to him because of an illness. That just wasn't his way. Besides, he was confident he would beat this disease and lead a long and happy life.

The wedding would take place on July 13, 2002 on Mount Hood, Oregon, but that wasn't the original choice. Since Brian's family lived in Baltimore, and since Kerri's family lived nearby in Pennsylvania, the original thought was to have a big wedding at the beach in Ocean City, Maryland. It would certainly be more convenient for the families, but there were a few challenges, like the summer crowds at the beach, and the potential logistical problems with places to stay, traffic, etc. Finally, Brian and Kerri realized they really were not that interested in a big formal wedding. Although they considered a destination wedding, they felt that would be too limiting and a significant expense for family and friends. They finally decided on a small wedding in Oregon with the idea that two to three months later, they could have a reception for family and friends back home in Baltimore where everyone could party, dance, and celebrate with Brian and Kerri.

Approximately sixty people flew out to Mt. Hood from the east coast for the wedding celebration. Brian and Kerri had planned a number of interesting events beginning on the Wednesday prior to the wedding. Most of the family and friends arrived on Wednesday or Thursday and were able to enjoy activities like hiking, golf, sightseeing, visiting a trout farm, taking a scenic drive through the Columbia River Gorge, or just plain relaxing and spending time with each other.

In Blase's case, he had one other important objective during this trip. By this time, he had been through two major surgeries: the removal of a carcinoid tumor from his left lung in September, 2001; and the removal of 70% of his liver in January, 2002. After the second surgery, it was pretty evident the cancer had spread, so Blase decided to seek out the leading doctors in the field of carcinoid cancer in order to make sure he was doing everything he could possibly do to beat the odds and overcome the disease. Ironically, the top expert in carcinoid cancer research was Dr. Larry Kvols from the Moffitt Research Center in Tampa, Florida, a two-hour drive from their winter home in Fort Myers. Blase first met Dr. Kvols in March, 2002. They bonded immediately, and from that point on, Dr. Kvols became his lead oncologist. Not one to leave a stone unturned, during his research, Blase also uncovered another leading expert in carcinoid cancer, Dr. Rodney Pommier, who just happened to practice at Oregon Health & Science University in Portland, about a thirty-minute drive from Brian's house in nearby Sandy, Oregon. On the Thursday before the wedding, Blase quietly visited with Dr. Pommier. He had previously sent him his medical history, and his objective was to see if there was anything in his latest research that might help. Dr. Pommier confirmed that everything Dr. Kvols was doing was exactly what he would be doing if Blase were his patient. He confirmed what Blase already knew—he had one of the best doctors available in Dr. Kvols.

The good news was Blase had the best specialists in the world to help him fight his battle. The bad news was that just a few months after his liver surgery, the latest test results indicated new tumors in his liver. Blase received this news a few weeks before the wedding. Dr. Kvols told Blase about a fairly new, non-invasive procedure called chemoembolization, which destroyed tumors by cutting off the oxygen supply. He planned to have this procedure soon after returning from the wedding.

On Friday, the day of the rehearsal dinner, the word started to leak out that Blase's cancer had continued to spread. Even though he had been through two major surgeries over the past nine months, he still looked very healthy. His biggest issue at that time was shortness of breath, due to missing a part of his lung. At this point, he had not yet had any chemo or radiation treatments and because he had such a positive outlook, we all thought the second surgery would result in complete success. Unfortunately, this was not the case.

Blase and the boys

Brian's wedding day

That evening, and for the remainder of the weekend, some tears were shed, but not by Blase, at least none that we could see. He continued to remain strong and positive. He refused to let his bad news overwhelm the love and happiness being shared with Brian and Kerri, and their family and friends. Somehow, the weekend was a complete success.

The following week, Brian and Kerri were off for a three-week honeymoon/vacation in Hawaii. About two weeks of that time was focused on Kerri playing in the Women's' World Ultimate Championship, which is why they chose Hawaii for their honeymoon destination. They obviously talked a lot about their future, and they both knew they wanted to be back closer to their families in Baltimore. They had already signed their teaching contracts for the upcoming school year. They also had a home that would need to be sold, and of course, they had Blase telling them not to worry about him and to live their lives. Before returning home from Hawaii, Brian and Kerri decided they would return to Baltimore after completing the school year the following June.

In March of 2003, Kerri became pregnant at about the same time Blase began his first round of chemotherapy. Brian and Kerri knew they had made the right decision. As it turned out, Blase was finalizing the purchase of Gratitude Farm in May, and it seemed to be the logical solution for Brian and Kerri to move into one of the homes on the property. Given their love for the outdoors, it made their transition from Oregon to Baltimore much easier. Brian was able to secure a teaching job with the Howard County School System and Kerri would soon become a stay-at-home mom.

Little Aja Rose was born in January 7, 2004 and was able to see Poppy often because they now lived close by. Blase loved seeing his grandchildren. No matter how good or bad he was feeling on a particular day, whenever he saw one of his grandchildren, he would feel better. On September 6, 2006, Aja met her new sister, Sofia Nicole. This was grandchild number four for Dawn and Blase. By the time Sofi was born, Blase had been diagnosed as a paraplegic and was relegated to a wheelchair. Blase held Sofi often. They would even fall asleep together. He would ride her around the house. Unfortunately, Aja Rose had reached the age where she couldn't understand why her poppy couldn't get out of the wheelchair to play with her. She didn't like the wheelchair, and Brian could sense that she was withdrawing a little from Blase. It was very sad to see.

Blase, Dawn, Aja, and Sofi

***

In April, 2006, about a month before Blase had his back surgery, he took the ten-minute drive over to Gratitude Farm to make a brief appearance at a crab feast/bachelor party for Andrew, the son of one of his best friends. He was also one of Blase's godsons. Blase was using a walker to get around, and his right leg was almost completely numb.

My Brother, My Keeper

He literally drove with his left foot. Dawn was out for the evening, and Blase was feeling pretty good. He really wanted to attend this event, but he had an ulterior motive. A number of people had heard the fiancée's father, like many fathers, was having some difficulty in making sure Andrew was the right choice for his daughter. That evening, when Blase met the father for the first time, he politely proceeded to tell this gentleman how fortunate he was to be getting such a wonderful and giving person as a son-in-law. He talked about Andrew's early years growing up, how many great friends he has, his tremendous success playing as a Division I lacrosse player in college, and most importantly, how much he loved his fiancée. Brian told me how proud he was to be there to hear his dad talk about Andrew's qualities. Blase expressed what many friends and family were feeling, but were perhaps unable to verbalize. Furthermore, he did it in a way that was positive and constructive rather than threatening or demeaning. Shortly after the discussion, Blase left the party. When he arrived back home, he somehow tripped as he tried to climb a step to get to the door and fell into some bushes. He struggled to get up, but he couldn't. After lying in the bushes for about twenty minutes, it occurred to him to push the panic button on his remote car key, and fortunately, one of his neighbors heard the alarm and was able to help him into the house.

About six weeks after the bachelor party, Andrew married his beautiful bride. Unfortunately, Blase was not able to attend because he was in intensive physical and occupational therapy resulting from his back operation. Had Blase been able to attend, he would have heard the father of the bride talk about how proud and happy he was to welcome his new son-in-law into the family.

This is just one of many examples of how Blase seemed to rise up to the occasion in order to right a wrong or help someone. Below is Brian's tribute, which clearly articulates what he learned from his hero, his dad.

141

Phil Cooke

Excerpt from Brian's Eulogy to Blase—October 5, 2007

JP Blase Cooke, Blase, the Blaser, Cooker, Cookie, Dad, Poppy.

We all knew my father by one of these names. Many of you had very special relationships with him and knew him in ways that I never will.

What I do know about my father? My father was a simple man. He prayed, took care of his health, worked hard, and loved harder.

There are many ways Dad lived a simple life. Today, I'm going to talk about his clothes. Dad had a habit of keeping clothes around way too long. We liked to sit around and watch TV after dinner, and for the first decade of my life, Dad would come home at around 7 PM, put his keys in their spot, read the mail he had brought in, sit with the family for dinner, then head upstairs to get out of his suit and put his comfies on. For that decade, his comfies of choice were an undershirt and a ratty old pair of yellow shorts that had holes in all the wrong places. Thank you, Mom, for eventually replacing those shorts. I remember a time in middle school, mid-'80s, digging around in Mom and Dad's closet and coming across a pair of classic, late-'60s blue bell bottom jeans. There were a couple of pairs, all neatly pressed and ready for a night out. (a night of dancing with friends maybe). I'd never seen these pants, but here they were, ready to go.

The way that my father treated his clothes says a lot about who he is and the way he treated people. He felt blessed for the clothes he had. He treated all of his clothes with respect. He never got rid of 'em or replaced them (Mom did that; together, they added many more to the closet). All of his clothes were dear to his heart.

My Brother, My Keeper

Those of you that know Dad know how important his Catholic faith was to him. Growing up, we all attended Catholic schools, never missed Sunday church followed by family breakfast, and on a daily basis, we watched a man live his life the way Jesus would. Right now, we're sitting in a church that Dad helped build.

He served on various boards here at St. Louis. The church next door (he helped build that one too) is where we as a family attended mass on Sundays, and the small chapel out front is where he attended mass often before work during the week. He was a devout Catholic and he has earned a VIP seat at the right hand of the Father.

My father was a health nut, a health fanatic. He took nutrition and exercise very seriously. He always paid attention to current information on various health trends in books, newspapers, magazines, and TV. As far back as I can remember, Dad would mix yogurt, granola, and various other powders, vitamins, blue-green algae, or whatever he might find to somehow make yogurt and granola even healthier. When he read salt was bad for him, he stopped using it. Same for butter. In my lifetime, he never smoked. He may have done it at a time, but when he heard it was bad for him, he was done.

Dad exercised every day. My father was an incredibly strong man, physically fit in every way; well, if you ever saw him bend over, you know he wasn't real flexible, but he worked on it. He followed a strict stretching routine for his back every morning for as long as he could, and he started yoga classes sometime in his late forties. Many of you played sports with my dad... softball, volleyball, tennis, racquetball, skiing (he was an awesome skier, but a broken leg while attempting a spread eagle (360 inverted) prevented him from pursuing his extreme skiing

143

passion. There was one other sport he loved to play . . . uh, which one am I missing? Oh, yeah, golf. Many of you played these sports with him and he <u>cherished</u> that time with you, especially those of you that lost money to him out on the golf course. He really loved y'all. He'd come home, giddy after playin', talking about beatin' so and so again, or takin' money from some young yuppie that thought he could beat Dad. I love y'all too. You see, Dad believed in sharing his winnings with us, so after comin' home from a big golf outing, he'd sometimes get us all together and give us our share of the winnings. He didn't ever keep a share for himself.

Dad worked harder than anyone I've ever known. The majority of my life, Dad left for work before 7 a.m. and arrived back home at 7 p.m. He didn't complain or talk much about work, he was more interested in what we had been up to. His work was never far away, though. No matter where we were, at home, on the beach, in an airplane, or at our sporting events, which Dad rarely missed, he would have a stack of papers in a file folder that he would peruse. He never missed what was going on around him and was quick to drop the papers when we came up to bat, but that folder was a constant in his life to the day he died. When we'd go out to various places, Dad would always point out jobs Harkins had built that were on the way to where we were headed; sometimes they were slightly out of the way, but when we'd pass the site or building, you could see the pride in his eyes as he'd slow down slightly and turn his head, trying to get a good look at his work in that passing moment.

Dad loved with all his heart and soul. Dad loved you unconditionally, Mom. You were his motivation, you were the foundation for his strength, and I never saw him happier than when he was with you. Kevin, Jason, and I know how much he loved us, he told us all the time. Dad loved his brothers, sisters, cousins, and in-laws. He was proud to be a member of this family, and each of you were very important to him. Dad loved his friends. He considered you and treated you like family. You were his source of escape from the daily grind. You kept him young and rejuvenated, and you inspired him to do great things. Dad loved Harkins. He dedicated most of his time on Earth to this company and he wouldn't have wanted to be anywhere else or with anyone else. Dad loved to help others. Being as blessed as he was, he felt obliged to help others whenever he could. He did it without expecting anything in return, but he often told us that in his experience, anything he gave, he got back, not just tenfold, but a hundredfold.

My father was an amazing man for many reasons. I feel truly honored to be one of the three people that got to call him Dad.

Memorandum

Date: September 4, 2008

To: All Employees

From: Blase Cooke

Re: THOUGHTS FOR THE DAY

"Many people will walk in and out of your life,
but only true friends will leave footprints in your heart.
To handle yourself, use your head;
to handle others, use your heart."

"Great minds discuss ideas,
average minds discuss events,
small minds discuss people."

"He who loses money loses much.
He who loses a friend loses much more.
He who loses faith loses all."

"Yesterday is history.
Tomorrow is a mystery.
Today is a gift."

Thanks to Gary Garofalo for these thoughts.

Chapter 9

Twentieth Annual Catholic Charities Golf Tournament— Baltimore Country Club, September 23, 2007

"He was a giant of a human being— passionately loving life, but always with his eye on the prize of his God and eternal life."

Hal Smith, December, 2007

Like the nineteen Catholic Charities Tournaments held previously, the twentieth was just as spectacular. It was a hot, beautiful sunny day in late September. The tournament was being played for the first time at Baltimore Country Club (BCC), perhaps the most famous and storied course in Baltimore. The club was founded in 1898 and hosted its first major USGA Golf tournament, the U.S. Open Championship, in 1899. I was told it was the first time Baltimore Country Club had ever closed both golf courses to hold a charity tournament. The tournament was being played just two weeks prior to BCC hosting the U.S. Mens' Senior Open, so the rough was high and the greens were fast—and both the East and West courses were in perfect condition (although I am told the rough is always high and the greens are always fast at BCC). The tournament had become so popular over the years, it had to be played at a golf club with two courses. There was only one thing missing that day—Blase. He was too ill to attend. But in spite of this, the twentieth Annual Catholic Charities Golf Tournament would still turn out to be one of his most memorable.

***

One of Blase's true passions in life was golf. His first taste of golf was as a caddy at the age of thirteen. He would get up early on Saturday mornings and hitchhike thirteen miles to Turf Valley Country Club, then spend the day carrying a couple of golf bags around the course. He would earn anywhere from $3 to perhaps $10 on a good day. Then he would hitchhike back home. Unlike today, in the early sixties, hitchhiking was considered a pretty safe way of getting around, and it was the only way to get to Turf Valley at 6:00 a.m. on a Saturday or Sunday morning.

There was a particular day, however, that pretty much ended his caddying career. One hot July day, Blase and one of his lifelong friends, Charlie Rose, were hitchhiking home after a prosperous day of caddying and were picked up by two guys, probably in their late teens or early twenties. When they stopped the car to pick up Blase and Charlie, the guy in the passenger seat jumped out and got in the back with Blase and told Charlie to sit up in the front seat. It seemed a bit weird to them, but Blase and Charlie were tired and it had been a long day. The good news was that these guys were going to drop them off very close to home.

They were in the car for about thirty seconds when suddenly, all hell broke loose. They heard a siren from a police car storming down the road, and instead of slowing down, the now very nervous driver floored it. Charlie, who was a quick thinker, asked the driver to drop him and Blase off at the next traffic light, and the guy looked at him and laughed. Then the guy in the back seat reached down on the floor and grabbed a machete and told everyone to sit tight and shut up. The cops were fast approaching, but the driver had no intention of stopping. The closer they got to the city, the more congested the traffic became, and the driver eventually ran into another car as he barreled through a traffic light. As soon as the car stopped, the two guys jumped out and tried to outrun the police, but they were apprehended quickly. Then Blase and Charlie, who had remained in the car, were quickly surrounded by cops with their guns drawn, and the guns were pointed at the frightened young caddies. With hands raised, they quickly explained to the officers they were innocent hitchhikers who were at the wrong place at the wrong time. They were told these guys had just stolen a car and had more than likely picked up Blase and Charlie to disguise their escape and to eventually rob them. Fortunately for Blase and Charlie, they returned home safely and with all their earnings for the day, and they had a story they both enjoyed sharing and exaggerating over many years. I believe the story above is as accurate as I can remember. Okay, so maybe the machete was really a penknife, but that's how it was told to me and that's how I remember it.

Blase started playing golf on a fairly regular basis not long after he was married in September 1968. He played at Forest Park Public Golf Course, a short, city-owned course. There were typically one or two foursomes who played early on Saturday mornings, arriving at the course around 6:30 a.m. and finishing by 11:00 a.m.

One would think playing golf early on a Saturday or Sunday morning would be a pretty safe endeavor. Oh, contraire. There were eight of us playing early one Sunday morning. It was about 9:00 a.m. and we had just hit our second shots toward the eleventh green of the short par four. The first foursome in our group of eight was just ahead of us, teeing off on the twelfth hole, a par three that was parallel to one of the many city streets surrounding the course. As we were coming off the green on our way to the par three twelfth hole, we first heard, then saw a car screeching around the corner with another car in hot pursuit. Suddenly, at least ten people, guys and girls, poured out of both cars, everyone yelling and arguing.

Meanwhile, a couple of us had hit our tee shots, and Blase was getting ready to hit when all the commotion started. He became a bit perturbed and was about to ask these folks to keep the noise down. Then we saw the gun. Yes, a guy named "Reds" had a gun, and was pointing it at the crowd of people. Actually, what we eventually concluded was he was pointing the gun at one person and the rest of the group was attempting to shield the person. We believe the tiff may have been related to a fight over a girl. At this point, the partygoers were only about fifty yards from where we were standing on the tee, so we very quickly completed our tee shots, picked up our pace, and after reaching the green, we declared all putts good and quickly moved on to the next tee.

We were now about an eight iron away from the group, and suddenly, Reds' soon-to-be victim decided to make a run for it, onto the golf course. Reds fired the pistol and shot the guy in the leg. Then everyone, except the victim who was bleeding in the fairway and one other guy, jumped into the cars and sped away. With all the commotion, I don't think they ever knew we were even there. Over the years, we had a lot of fun playing at Forest Park, but that was definitely one of our most memorable rounds of golf.

In the late seventies, Blase became a member of Turf Valley Golf and Country Club, the course where he first learned about the game as a caddy. This is also where Blase introduced his sons to the game. Blase's favorite foursome of all consisted of him and his boys. He always carried a picture of his favorite foursome in his wallet.

Blase and boys, his favorite foursome

Blase loved golf trips, from Myrtle Beach to Pebble Beach, to Ireland, Scotland, and many others great venues. One of his lifelong goals was to play the top one hundred courses in the world, and he played quite a few. He was very grateful to have the opportunity to play courses like Pine Valley, Merion, Winged Foot, Congressional, Oakmont, St. Andrews, Ballybunion, and Royal County Down, among many others.

Blase in Bally Bunion, Ireland

From the early eighties until his last round of golf in early 2006, Blase participated in, and typically arranged, many memorable golf outings. There was the infamous Polish Open, which was started by one of Blase's great friends, Pete Twardaweicz. The tournament was played every October in Ocean City, MD, and was filled with laughs from beginning to end.

In the spring, it was the annual five-day trip to Myrtle Beach, loosely organized by David and Patrick Carney, who had known and loved

Blase since they were teenagers. Although David and Patrick worked hard every winter to identify the courses we would play, where we would stay, etc., it was Blase who always seemed to take charge in organizing the actual event.

As golf trips go, this one was pretty involved because there were twenty-four players. About a third of the people would fly, so Blase would constantly stay on David to get the dates and arrangements confirmed early so he could get the cheapest and most convenient flights for the guys who were flying down from Baltimore to Myrtle Beach. Then he would work with another friend, Alex Loehman, to create the foursomes for each day, which would include the course we would be playing, who we were playing with, handicaps, and a myriad of other things to keep things organized and fun. Blase and Alex developed the tournaments we played and would collect the $100 prize money from everyone. Blase would then become the "bank" and would take charge of paying out the winners.

Blase and buddies in Myrtle Beach, 1996

It's not easy to get twenty-four guys to listen or hear anything, especially when you are trying to get all of them to a golf course at 7:00 a.m. Even though we played the same tournament formats over a twenty-year period, it was always amazing to Blase that every spring he would need to explain the tournament rules again and again, even though the rules rarely changed. The golf was always fun, very competitive, and hotly contested. Each day would include both individual and team events, so there were lots of ways to try to win your original investment and then some. However, winning money wasn't what this trip was about. In fact, Blase designed his tournament to include a handicap adjustment to enable guys who were playing poorly to have a better chance of winning an individual prize on the next day.

Over the many years he journeyed to Myrtle Beach, Blase won often. He was a very good golfer, a ten-handicapper, a really good ten-handicapper. I believe the lowest handicap he ever held was a seven. Whenever the chips were down and the pressure was on and he really needed to make a clutch shot or putt, he always seemed to come through, especially in the team events. One of the reasons he won often in the team events was because he always set goals for the team and he got everyone to believe they could win. If one of the players was not having a good day, he would encourage them to keep trying. It was amazing how he was able to motivate his team to victory, and when he won, he shared his winnings by picking up a dinner tab. In fact, he would pick up a tab even when he didn't win.

In addition to golf, there was also a lot of card playing—poker, gin, and pitch. Boy, did that trip fly by! We literally chuckled and laughed continuously for five days. We also found time to talk about life and death, family, kids, parents, and grandparents. We didn't spend much time at all talking about our jobs because this trip was all about getting away and relaxing for a little while. We talked about how grateful we were to be in a position to enjoy our male bonding adventure, and we developed lifelong friendships with a bunch of great guys. Thanks to a gentle reminder from Blase, we also found time to get to church and to thank God for our treasured time away.

Blase's last Myrtle Beach trip was in 2004. He was about three years into his fight with cancer, and he realized he could no longer handle the physical challenge of playing five days in a row. Everyone wanted him to come even if he couldn't play, or if he could only play every other day, but Blase refused. It was a golf trip, and he was not interested in being a burden. As much as he wanted to be there, and as much as we wanted him to be there, he was just not interested in going if he couldn't handle the trip—end of story.

We found out pretty quickly that our annual Myrtle Beach trip just wasn't the same without Blaser. We sort of meandered through the next two years. We still laughed, but not as much. The annual World Series of Poker event, which Blase loved, didn't happen. Our leader and our motivator was out of action, and at some level, we all felt it; we all missed him, and we all talked about him.

Our annual trip lasted for twenty years, seventeen years with Blase and three years without him. Our twentieth and final trip was in April, 2007, six months before Blase died. After every trip, Blase would always send out a letter to all the players summarizing the trip. He even sent out letters during the years he wasn't able to attend. Below is an excerpt from one of his many letters.

Memorandum

Date: August 10, 2003

To: Myrtle Beach Golf Participants

From: Blase Cooke

Re: MYRTLE BEACH 2003 FINAL RECAP

Day 1	Team	Score
First Place	Ben Civiletti, Glenn Cooke, Tom Booth, Bob Weiss	-19
Second Place	Chris Burns, Joe Heaps, Alex Lohmann, "Ole Yeller" Montgomery	-18
Third Place	Tom Burns, Rod Compton, Dave Carney, Ron Regan	-17

Day 2	Team	Score
First Place	Blase Cooke, Joe Heaps, Charlie Rose, Don Reuwer	-23
Second Place	Ben Civiletti, Patrick Carney, Dave Carney, Billy Vaselaros	-20
Third Place	Chris Burns, Ralph Updike, Jim Campbell, Ron Regan	-18

Day 3	Team	Score
First Place	Phil Cooke, Joe Heaps, Dave Carney, Vic Marone	-27
Second Place	Tom Burns, Ralph Updike, Tom Booth, Billy Vaselaros	-20
Third Place	Blase Cooke, Patrick Carney, Alex Lohmann, Ron Regan	-19

As you can see from the recap of the scoring, one stroke separated winners from losers. Consequently, we could each imagine how many bad shots and short putts cost us the tournament.

Congratulations to Joe "Franey" Heaps, who was the overall individual winner, as well as a winner each day in the team competition. It still amazes me that a seventy-year-old B-player can beat every A player every day. Also, congratulations to Glenn Cooke, who finished in fourth place and had his best overall year ever— because he did not show up on the first day! Ben and Blase had the most consistent scores, whereas Tom and Glenn surged on the last day to pass Patrick, Alex, Bippy, and the Burns brothers, who were all in the money. Unfortunately, Alex went from well into first place to third place with a smooth 102—by far his worst score of the tournament.

David had another poor trip with golf, but made up for it in cards. However, Billy beat David in golf in both score and bets every day, which made Billy happier than winning the whole tournament.

Congratulations to the winning Ryder Cup team, Fran Heaps, Blase, Ben, Rod, Ralph, George, Patrick, Campo, David, Rego, Redbird, and Don, who literally won by half a point. If any of the close

My Brother, My Keeper

matches from the B team would have won one hole their way and gained them that extra half-point, the match would have been dead even. This is the closest Ryder Cup ever, and everyone agrees that it was a great competition.

There are numerous memorable occasions from every trip and I would like to cite just a few from this one.

1. *The best comment of the week was Chris Burns, who was playing with Charlie, Rod, and Bob. The Ranger was putting a lot of pressure on them to keep up and Chris stated he was playing with a seventy-year-old, a person with a bad hip, and a person with one arm, and how could he possibly do anything to keep them up? The Ranger did not bother Chris anymore, and started bothering me because one of our players was somewhat deliberate.*
2. *Charlie committed the biggest renege in the history of the game of pitch when he did not play an ace of spades on the first trick. We all hope your hip is feeling better.*
3. *Everyone has some suspicion that Dave Carney wins at pitch all of the time because he beats everyone with the pencil, as well as his extraordinary card skills. Alex picked up that Dave was only keeping score for three teams in a four-team game, which convinced us that Dave really doesn't know how to keep score.*
4. *Congratulations to Ralph, who won the World Series of Poker, to Campo for coming in second and PhilBoy in third. Finally, the best poker player won this tournament. Dave, who did not have the opportunity to keep score, was the first one eliminated of the twelve players.*
5. *Patrick started off with his best year ever and was winning the tournament going into the third day, when he did not make one single par for our team. He also severely affected my game, which was minus one after five holes when he*

157

jumped and screamed like a little girl when he saw a snake in the woods. I proceeded to go plus ten on the next six holes because I was so upset.

6. *Don Reuwer was a good addition to the group and it was nice having Rod Compton back again. The luck of the draw the first day had Glenn cashing big tickets and Frank coming in last. Red Dog was seen consulting with Charlie about hip replacement, and it was very refreshing not to hear Campbell whining too much this year because he played so well.*

7. *Ron Regan is the most improved golfer, and I predict he will be out of the last group next year and Dave Carney will be back in it.*

A special thanks to Alex Lohmann, PhilBoy, and Kevin for helping me do the scoring and auditing the final results.

I would like to thank all of my partners for their extraordinary play and the good competition from everyone. Thanks for making this another extremely memorable trip for me. I very much look forward to seeing everyone on this trip again next year.

Until then, have a good life, play good golf, and be well.

As a result of his success in business, and given the fact that many of Blase's business friends and partners loved golf, Blase began organizing golf trips to more exotic places like Pebble Beach, Bandon Dunes, Ireland, and Scotland. I am told some business was conducted on these trips, but they were really focused on competing, having fun, and getting to know one another outside of the business atmosphere.

Blase at Royal County Down, Ireland, 1998

One of Blase's closest friends, Theo Rogers, president of A&R Companies, has been both a client and friend since 1980. Theo's story below about their relationship is typical of the impact Blase had on people.

Our relationship was based on complete trust in each other. A&R has done over $250 million in construction with Harkins, and in the twenty-seven years that the work has spanned, we never had an issue that took more than five minutes to resolve. Our philosophy was based on "You take care of me and I'll

*take care of you," meaning that if things did not go well for
you, I will take part of the pain, and vice-versa. That
philosophy has also been accepted by the current leadership at
Harkins.*

*When Blase and I went on our many golf trips around the
world, we had a ritual: we would sit next to each other on the
plane, and both of us would present our "issues" listed on an
index card for discussion. In every instance, all issues were
resolved before the plane became airborne. Then the real issues
could be discussed, i.e., how many strokes were being given and
what was the betting matrix.*

*It has become legend in the local development/construction
community that A&R and Harkins completed a $50 million
development without a contract. It was only after the project
was completed that we decided that we should have a contract
to satisfy our accountants. I don't know many entities that have
that level of trust in each other.*

*There are many compelling personal events that I shared with
Blase that I shall always hold dear. Blase was my hero, both as
a businessman and as a human being. I can only hope to be
like him.*

***

The First Annual Catholic Charities Golf Tournament was held on
September 27, 1987 at Avenel Country Club in Potomac, Maryland.

Blase was approached by Hal Smith, the executive director of Catholic
Charities, who asked him if he would put together a charity golf
tournament to raise some money. He realized he could leverage his love
of golf to help the needy and those less fortunate, and he wanted to raise

a lot of money, so he persuaded the other members of the newly organized golf committee to create a tournament with an individual entry fee of one thousand dollars per person. The goal was to offer a world-class golf event at a world-class venue, and most importantly, to let everyone know this event was making a difference in people's lives.

The tournament was an all-day event, which included breakfast, lunch, golf, a cocktail hour, dinner, and the awarding of the various individual and team winners. There were also a number of very nice raffle prizes, but there was a catch: you had to be there to win. Perhaps the most important and touching part of the entire day was Hal's after dinner talk and presentation, which would highlight one of the many wonderful services provided by Catholic Charities. This, of course, happened before the raffle prizes to ensure that everyone would stay, which enabled them to see and hear real stories of real people who were turning their lives around. And once you heard one of Hal's beautiful and inspirational presentations, you would look forward to next year to hear another touching story. The attendees were very privileged to have retired Archbishop William Borders, who not only played or participated in all twenty tournaments, but who was also the first to send in his check every year. We were also privileged to have his Eminence, William Cardinal Keeler, speak at almost every event as well. I can't tell you how many times people would say that it was the best charity tournament they had ever attended.

Over the years, Blase and his devoted team of board members would make sure every tournament was as good as it could be. They found new ways to raise money by developing new golf events and coming up with some creative auctions. There was the Ryder Cup event, which brought together companies and individuals who would play a match play tournament for a designated Catholic charity organization, and they developed a young professionals' golf outing, which encouraged young businessmen and entrepreneurs to give back to their community through charitable giving. Both of these events continue to this day.

With regard to creative auctions, there is one particular auction which comes to mind, and it occurred at the second Catholic Charities Golf Tournament back in 1988. Like most avid golfers, Blase always had a desire to play at Augusta. During the banquet that year, Hal Smith and the folks at Catholic Charities awarded Blase an open invitation to play at Augusta. But instead of fulfilling one of his lifelong golf dreams, he decided to auction off his invitation that evening to the highest bidder. Many years later, in 2003, as a result of his continued work with the tournament, he received yet another invitation. Unfortunately, due to other priorities, scheduling issues, and his rapidly declining health, he never got to play there.

Through Blase's leadership, he was able to combine his love of golf and his desire to help others in need to create an event that raised over two million dollars over a twenty-year period. Even with his passing, it will continue to grow and prosper. Shortly after Blase passed, the Catholic Charities Board honored him by renaming the tournament the J.P. Blase Cooke Memorial Catholic Charities Golf Tournament.

As mentioned earlier, what was to be Blase's final Catholic Charities Tournament took place on September 23, 2007, just two weeks before he died. Blase was too ill to even attend the twentieth anniversary of the event. However, he was well represented by two of his sons, Jason and Kevin, and there is no doubt he was definitely there in spirit. It turns out that, had Blase been healthy enough to play, he would have played on a winning team on BCC's most famous and challenging East Course. The team included two of his sons and two of his senior executives from Harkins Builders, Gary Garofalo and Dick Lombardo.

The key performer in the group that day was not Dick or Gary, who are both excellent low-handicap golfers, or Kevin, who played golf on his high school and college teams, but Blase's firstborn son, Jason. Ironically, Jason doesn't play a lot of golf. With two young

162

children at home and a pretty hectic business schedule, he does not have the luxury of spending four to five hours on a golf course either during the week or on weekends. In fact, he had only played a few rounds the entire year, so he certainly wasn't expecting to have the round of his life—but he did. Jason's incredible play inspired his teammates to a runaway victory. Jason also won one of the longest drive contests. When Blase heard the news, he was ecstatic and very proud of both "his" team and his sons. I wouldn't be surprised if he didn't try to get a few bets lined up with some of his other buddies who were playing that day, and I'm sure Blase was a key ingredient to their victory because he was definitely there in spirit. He could no longer play golf, or even walk for that matter, but he still probably played the entire round of golf that day in his imagination. He was there, right beside his team, offering encouragement and support. Blase was, and still is, the heart and soul of this tournament, and will be for many years to come.

That evening, both Jason and Kevin made their dad proud again by representing him at the awards event. Kevin read a letter from Blase on his behalf and Jason offered the following remarks.

Jason's Remarks to the Golf Participants

It is an honor to be here with you tonight, and it is especially an honor to be here representing my father, Blase Cooke. Hal asked me to talk a little about Blase for those who might not know him.

I consider myself very lucky to have not only a father, but a friend, a mentor, role model, and a hero.

As a father, he is always there with a hug and encouraging words, and as much as he loves being a father, he loves being a grandfather or "Poppy."

As a friend, I've learned the importance and power of friendship through watching how he interacted with others. He also never forgot where he came from and those he grew up with.

As a mentor, I have seen how he enjoys sharing his knowledge and insight with anyone who asked him, and I have had numerous people tell me how he has made a difference in their lives.

As a role model, he has never shied away from a leadership position and commits himself to excellence in business, life, and charity.

And as my hero, he has shown a passion for life and everything he does, especially during his greatest challenge, battling cancer for the past six-and-a-half years, he does not complain or bring others down. He stays positive and fights to get better every day.

I want to thank all of you for being here today to support Catholic Charities. Your participation today is the continuation of the vision that Hal and Blase shared over twenty years ago.

Now I would like to ask my brother, Kevin, to read a letter that Blase wanted us to share with all of you.

***

Blase's Letter to the Golf Participants

Hi, Fellow Golf Guys:

Thank you so much for your support over the past twenty years, and it's wonderful to have our twentieth anniversary at Baltimore Country Club.

My Brother, My Keeper

Some of you know my definition of a "golf guy." He is someone you enjoy being with, not only on the golf course, but sharing a meal together, sharing a prayer, sharing a family event, a card game, and openly discussing everything including politics and religion. A lot of guys that play golf are not "golf guys" because they don't follow the strict rules of golf or are not the type of person you enjoy being around. Bill Clinton plays golf (pause), but he is certainly not a "golf guy."

It's hard to believe that Hal talked me into chairing this committee, which started out to be around forty Catholic leaders—to play golf together, get to know one another, and raise a little money for Catholic Charities. I don't believe Hal or I could have imagined us growing to 232 players, which has been our goal for the past several years. At the time, the committee knew this was a reach goal, but I like to say it's better to set the bar high and just miss than set it too low and hit it.

We have some individuals and two companies that have supported us all twenty years and they are as follows:

> *Archbishop Borders - he is one of my heroes and his check is the first one in every year.*
> *Craig Birmingham*
> *Bill Franey*
> *Mike Monaghan*
> *Theo Rodgers*
> *John Souder*
> *Franey, Parr, and Muha*
> *Harkins Builders*

Would the people mentioned and the representatives Franey, Parr, and Muha and Harkins Builders here this evening please stand, and let's give them a round of applause.

Phil Cooke

I'd very much like to be with you this evening to celebrate this significant milestone and congratulate each of you in person. Unfortunately, my health keeps me away another year, but God willing, I'll be back next year.

Many thanks to Fran Contino, Hal Smith, Amy Ciarlo, and the entire committee for their extraordinary efforts in selling out this year's event. It has been a pleasure working with you as well as the many other previous committee members, volunteers, and staff. The success of this tournament is a tribute to all of them and each of you here this evening. One of the great benefits in charitable and nonprofit involvement is meeting so many terrific people—many of whom are here this evening. I am blessed to have friendships with so many wonderful people that I wouldn't know if not for involvement in charitable work. From the bottom of my heart, thank you, thank you, thank you.

The very best to each of you. May our good Lord continue to guide and bless all of you and your families.

Blase

***

Hal Smith and Blase developed a very special bond over the years, and that relationship has resulted in improving many lives of the less fortunate in the Baltimore area. In 1998, Catholic Charities was celebrating its seventy-fifth anniversary and Hal came up with an outstanding fund raising idea—a dragon boat race which would take place in Baltimore's Inner Harbor. A dragon boat is a canoe-like boat which holds twenty paddlers, a drummer, and a steersman, with colorful dragon heads and tails on either end. The event itself promotes competition, teamwork, and harmony. Hal approached Blase to see if his company would be interested in becoming a participating sponsor for the event and he immediately said yes. Like the Catholic Charities Golf Tournament, he saw this event as an excellent way to promote teamwork and camaraderie within his own company, to bring together other major businesses in Baltimore to help the community, and to raise money for one of his favorite charities. This was a no-brainer in Blase's book.

Keep in mind that committing to an event like this requires that a company bring together a significant number of employees who would commit to training a team of rowers, practicing, and attending the all-day event. This is not a trivial thing. Below is the schedule for the 2008 event from the Catholic Charities website, which gives an idea of the level of effort involved:

Dragon Boat Timeline

January/April 2008
Official sponsorship packets will be presented through February.

April/May, 2008
Prepare! It's time to start the "buzz" in you company—show the video, distribute flyers, and begin to assemble team members. The key is to get as many people involved in all of the pre-race activities. Appoint a team captain and team liaison for your dragon boat team, and assemble your team spirit committee. It's a great time to meet with your Catholic Charities partner program to help chart your course over the next few months.

May/June, 2008
Team building! Now is the time to formalize your teams—both in and out of the water. Plan to attend the team captains' meeting, where you'll get additional details and information regarding all pre-race and race day activities. Continue to work with your partner program to held build excitement for a very spirited race day!

July/August, 2008
Practice, practice, practice! On water, your team will attend weekly practices at The Canton Marine Center under the supervision of our coaching staff. On land, your team spirit committee will be in full gear, developing the team chant, designing the tent decorations, and adding the final touches to the team hat.

Saturday, September 13, 2008
RACE DAY! Invite your friends, family, and all of your employees for a day of fun, festivities, and excitement as you cheer on your team in the Inner Harbor.

***

The first event in 1998 had nine corporations participate. Under Blase's leadership, Harkins Builders took third place in the inaugural event. Blase always liked to point out that, although they didn't win the actual event, they were awarded first place for the "best dragon boat chant." As the CEO, Blase could have easily said yes to Hal, sign the sponsorship check, and then recruit one of his employees to make it happen. But that's not how Blase operated. He personally got involved. He led by example. He recruited employees and set goals. He encouraged the team to practice and hone their skills so they would be prepared to win, and he actively participated because he was the drummer for the team for a number of years.

Since the first event in 1998, the dragon boat has become a favorite within the Baltimore community and has become a premier biennial corporate event. Every year, the maximum number of thirty-three corporate teams sign up to participate, including companies like Verizon, T. Rowe Price, *The Baltimore Sun*, Constellation Energy, M&T Bank, Legg Mason, and of course, Harkins Builders. Even the Baltimore City Police and Fire Departments enter the event. Hal's idea is now generating approximately $500,000 annually to help Catholic

Charities help those in need in the Baltimore area, and it all started when one guy, Blase Cooke, told another guy, Hal Smith, count me in.

Blase leading his dragon boat team, 1998

In addition to sharing a personal friendship and a desire to help others, they also shared a strong faith in God. Below is reflection from Hal on Blase's passing.

Blase had a real passion for life and living it to the fullest, seizing life every minute of every day. He never took anything for granted, whether it be his good fortune in life or the quality necessary to make sure a job was done right. He took personal responsibility for everything that happened around him and had supreme confidence that he could make things come out right in the end, from golf scores to building a company. The fact that he had goals for the future didn't detract him from his ability to live in the present and fully experience the present moment, even when he was battling through the last few months of his illness.

*Blase made a number of significant gifts to the fundraising
effort of Catholic Charities in response to specific requests I
made to him. He responded positively to every one. Many times
in fundraising, people want to know at what level other people
are giving in order to calculate how much they should give. Not
Blase. He always gave what he thought was right without
regard to what other people did. By doing this, he made it
possible to use his gift as a leadership inspirational guide to
encourage others to make a gift larger than they otherwise
might have done. He knew we not only needed his gift, but his
leadership to go first to bring others to a significant gift. He
was a giant of a human being—passionately loving life, but
always with his eye on the prize of his God and eternal life. I
miss him dearly.*

***

One of Blase's personal/family goals was to own a home on a golf
course. In 1990, he achieved this lifelong dream and built a beautiful
home overlooking the seventh hole of Cattail Creek Country Club in
Glenwood, MD. He was one of the founding members of Cattail
Creek and had served on the Board of Directors from the club's
inception in 1990 until he resigned in 2001. He also served as the
executive vice president from 1995–1997 and president of the Club
from 1997–1999.

Cattail holds a special place in Blase's heart. He developed a great
number of friendships with so many of his golfing buddies, and for
many of them, those friendships extended well beyond the golf course.
Because of his illness, his last round of golf was in February, 2006.
From that point on, he would spend most of his waking hours in his
family room overlooking the seventh hole. Occasionally, when the
weather was nice, he would sit out on his deck and watch the golfers

as they played, dreaming of the day when he would be back playing with his buddies again.

Perhaps the most poignant memory from Cattail Creek came in the summer of 2007. Cattail was hosting its annual Member/Guest Tournament, which was one of Blase's favorite golf events. He last played in the tournament in 2005. On the final day of the event, just after the 144 golfers finished lunch, and before they were to start their final nine-hole match, one of his friends, Chris Spendley, suggested they ride out to the seventh hole to wish him well. They first called over to his house and asked Dawn if he was feeling well enough to come out on the deck. After hearing the plan, Dawn knew that no matter how well or bad he felt, he was going to feel much better when he was greeted by the throng of well-wishers. So she didn't even tell him, she just rolled him out onto the deck.

A few minutes later, the seventh fairway was enveloped with golf carts and golfers. Practically every player took the time to come out to wish him well. They were yelling out and waving. Then a few friends came up to give him a hug and share a personal thought. The next thing he knew, practically everyone, even people who had never met Blase, but perhaps heard about him on the ride out, came up to personally greet him. Blase was humbled by the outpouring of love and good words from so many, and his response was, "I hope to be playing with you in this event next year."

A few months later, Blase died peacefully in his home overlooking the seventh hole at Cattail Creek Country Club.

Memorandum

To: All Employees

From: Blase Cooke

Re: **THOUGHTS FOR THE DAY**

"Those who preserve their integrity remain unshaken by the storms of daily life. They do not stir like leaves on a tree or follow the herd where it runs. In their mind remains the ideal attitude and conduct of living. This is not something given to them by others, it is their roots—it is a strength that exists deep within them."

Anonymous Native American

"Believe in yourself. You gain strength, courage, and confidence by every experience in which you stop to look fear in the face—you must do that which you think you cannot do."

Eleanor Roosevelt

"Successful is the person who has lived well, laughed often, and loved much, who has gained the respect of children, who leaves the world better than they found it, who has never lacked appreciation for the Earth's beauty, who never fails to look for the best in others or give the best of themselves."

Robert Louis Stevenson

"Watch your thoughts, for they become words. Choose your words, for they become actions. Understand your actions, for they become habits. Study your habits, for they will become your character. Develop your character, for it becomes your destiny."

Frank Outlaw

My Brother, My Keeper

"This is the beginning of a new day. You have been given this day to use as you will. You can waste or use it for good. What you do today is important because you are exchanging a day of your life for it. When tomorrow comes, this day will be gone forever; in its place is something that you have left behind—let it be something good."

Author Unkown

"I expect to pass through this world but once. Any good I can do, or any kindness that I can show, let me do now, for I shall not pass this way again."

Stephan Grellet

Chapter 10

Kevin's Wedding—Chautauqua, New York, June 10, 2006

"That's the kind of stuff Blase was made of—tough, determined, courageous and persevering, but always optimistic."

J.P. Bolduc, November 20, 2007

June 10, 2006 was a beautiful sunny day in Chautauqua, NY. This area of western New York state is known for the Chautauqua Institution, which was founded in 1874. The Chautauqua Institution is a not-for-profit, 750-acre educational center nestled beside Chautauqua Lake. Approximately 7,500 people reside there during the summer season, and over 140,000 attend scheduled public events throughout the year. Over 8,000 students enroll annually in the Chautauqua Summer School, which offers courses in art, music, dance, theater, writing skills, and a wide variety of special interests. The institution was designated a National Historic Landmark on June 30, 1989.

Chautauqua Institution also happens to be a beautiful place for a wedding, and since Kate Prechtl, Kevin's fiancée, had spent almost every summer living there, it was the obvious place to formally begin the celebration of her new life with Kevin. Kate's dad, Greg, has run the Boys' and Girls' Club at Chautauqua for the past twenty-two years. The Prechtl family has many fond memories of their summers in Chautauqua, and it was anticipated that this wedding weekend would most definitely become one of the best.

How did a really sweet girl from upstate New York ever find the young party animal from Baltimore? Well, of course, at a party that Kevin had crashed, which was pretty typical for Kevin. In February 2002, Kevin had decided to move back from Ashland, Oregon to be closer to his dad. He had been living with Brian for about two years. They both really enjoyed the mountainous outdoor lifestyle Ashland provided, especially the skiing and snowboarding on Mt. Hood. Kevin liked Oregon so much that he was seriously considering making Ashland his permanent home, but sometimes life can take an unexpected turn. After Blase's recent liver surgery, Kevin sensed that things were getting much more serious with his dad. Blase had talked often with both of his sons living in Oregon, and of course, when they asked how he was doing, he always told them he was doing TERRIFIC, and then he would turn his attention to each of them to find out how they were doing. During that conversation in February, Kevin knew the cancer had gotten the better of him because he did not hear the word "terrific" that day. He knew the time had come for him to return home. One could conclude that had Blase never had cancer, and had Kevin never moved back to Baltimore, he and Kate would never have met. It's amazing how one event in someone's life, positive or negative, can have such a dramatic impact, not only on his own life, but on those of so many others.

***

Kate had moved to Baltimore in 2000 after graduating from Miami of Ohio and began teaching elementary school in Annapolis. In July 2003, Kate decided to throw a barbecue party and Kevin convinced a friend of his to let him tag along. When Kevin met Kate, he was instantly attracted to her. During their first conversation, they quickly realized they had something in common in that they both shared the same birthday, September 8. Normally when Kevin met a girl he was attracted to, he would immediately ask her out on a date. In the case of Kate, it was clearly different. He did two things he had never done before. That night, he told his sister-in-law, Alexis, he thought he had just met the person he would marry. Then he wrote her a letter. He thanked her for throwing the party. He wrote how he enjoyed the many things they had discussed that evening, and he told her he was very interested in seeing her again. In today's Internet-savvy world, this was clearly a very unusual thing for a person like Kevin, or any Generation X person to do. A "Gen-X" person would be more apt to send a quick text message or email, or even a quick cell phone call, but certainly not a letter delivered via the U.S. Postal Service. I know Kevin didn't realize this at the time, but I now find it more than a coincidence he used this particular form of communication. Blase was well known for his written notes to people. He would be the first to tell you he was not a techie. The closest Blase came to using technology was an audio recorder. Thanks to Joani, his audio messages were transformed into written notes, or if he was communicating with larger groups of people, emails. Perhaps Kevin knew his next communication with Kate was very important, so he did something special by writing the note, and perhaps he subconsciously made the decision to write the note as a result of one of his dad's good habits. Sometimes we do and say things and we aren't sure why we have the impulse. Maybe it comes from a lesson from a school teacher from long ago, or from a parent, or perhaps from a guardian angel.

In any case, the letter must have worked, because the next step in the courtship came from Kate. About a month later, Kate ran into Kevin when she was out with a couple of friends. During the conversation, she found out Kevin had spent some time in Oregon. The following Sunday was a gorgeous summer day, and Kate wanted to take a hike. She thought of Kevin, assuming that a guy who lived in Oregon probably liked to hike, so she decided to give him a call, but before doing so, she called her mom for some advice. She told her mom she had met a guy who had crashed her party the month before, then wrote her a letter, and she was thinking of asking him to take a walk in the woods with her! Of course, her mom said yes. Looking back, both Kate and her mom, Linda, laugh about how mom permitted her daughter to go out into the woods with someone she hardly knew. Thank goodness, everything worked out fine, and from that point on, the courtship began in earnest.

177

Birthdays were a very special family tradition for Blase, Dawn, and their sons. For as long as Kevin could remember, every birthday for each son was a special dinner with Mom and Dad at the restaurant of their choosing. It was very special time when Jason, Brian, and Kevin could talk directly with their mom and dad about their individual hopes and dreams. As Kevin's twenty-sixth birthday approached, he decided since Kate's birthday was on the same day, perhaps they would all share it together. Although Kevin had just recently begun dating Kate, Blase and Dawn were fine with the request, and knowing Kevin had never had a serious relationship with a girl, in the back of their minds, they suspected this meant something much more than just bringing a date out for a dinner.

When Kevin asked Kate to go out to dinner to meet his mom and dad, the first thing she did was call her mom again. This was only their third or fourth date, and already Kevin wanted Kate to meet his mom and dad? And again, Kate's mom approved the request (maybe she sensed something as well) and Kate met Blase and Dawn for the first time. Kate had two distinct memories from that evening. Shortly after they arrived at the restaurant, the waiter brought over a bottle of champagne from a friend of Blase's who had heard he would be celebrating Kevin's birthday. Kate thought, who is this guy that someone would send a rather expensive bottle of champagne? The funny thing was Blase didn't drink. But the second memory was the most vivid. Had Kate not been told Blase had been fighting cancer for more than three years, she would have never known he even had cancer. Both physically and mentally, he seemed perfectly normal. Dawn and Kevin clearly saw significant changes in Blasé, but Kate simply could not see it. She had nothing to compare it to because this was the first time they had ever met. Like anyone in her position, Kate was expecting to see a sick person. This was a tremendous testimony to Blase's strength and determination to not let the cancer beat him, to not let it get in the way of what was really important to him—his family and this beautiful young lady who would one day be a significant part of it.

My Brother, My Keeper

The relationship and love between Kevin and Kate continued to grow. They had been dating for almost a year. Kevin had made several trips with Kate to visit her parents in upstate New York. Because family was so important to both Kate and Kevin, they wanted their parents to meet, so in June 2004, Kate invited her parents and Blase and Dawn to get together. They decided to have everyone meet at Kate's apartment in Annapolis for appetizers and then head out for dinner at a local restaurant. The plan was to spend an hour or so getting to know each other before going to the restaurant. Unfortunately, Greg and Linda's trip from Buffalo took longer than expected, and there was very little time for everyone to get better acquainted beforehand. As soon as everyone was seated at the restaurant, the only two people not talking were Kate and Kevin. Before you knew it, Dawn and Linda and Blase and Greg were deeply involved in conversation. Within fifteen minutes, Greg and Blase were in tears because they realized they had very similar backgrounds, interests, and beliefs. They shared stories about their families, their kids, and the deaths of their parents—they bonded even faster than Kevin and Kate did! Toward the end of a wonderful evening, Blase suddenly dropped a bombshell from out of the blue: "So you have us all here tonight. Do you have an announcement? Are you getting engaged?" Greg immediately wondered if Blase knew something he didn't. Keep in mind Kate was the oldest of three children, none of whom were married, so Greg had never been through this before. By this time, Blase was a pro at the wedding gig, since his two older sons were married and had kids already, and more importantly, Blase realized what an amazing catch Kate would be for Kevin. There was no question Blase wanted Kevin to seal the deal as soon as possible. Greg, on the other hand, was thinking, I like Kevin, but he has only known Kate for a year. What's going on? Aren't we moving a little too fast? Even Kevin was at a loss for words, which to my knowledge, had never happened before. Finally, Kevin found the words he was looking for—check please, which were two words I had never heard Kevin say before.

No one got engaged that evening, but preparations were underway. At the end of 2004, Kevin celebrated the New Year with the Prechtl family in Chautauqua. He knew he was ready to ask Greg for Kate's hand, but he didn't know exactly when or how he was going to do it. About midway through the weekend visit, Kate and her mom decided to make a run to the grocery store, and Kevin seized the moment to ask Greg for permission to marry his daughter. Greg responded by telling Kevin he didn't need to ask permission because nobody did that anymore. He then proceeded to grill him on how he was going to take care of his daughter and provide for her. Now that Kevin had the official approval to proceed, the next obvious question was, when would he ask Kate?

It was April 23, 2005, the night of the My Brother's Keeper tribute to Blase, and Blase was making his remarks after receiving the award. The first thing he did, of course, was acknowledge his lovely wife, Dawn, Jason and his wife, Alexis, Brian and his wife, Kerri, his four beautiful grandchildren, and Kevin and Kate. He paused for a moment and then wondered out loud why Kevin had not yet asked Kate for her hand—in front of more than 1,000 people. At the time, Blase didn't know Kevin had received permission from Greg to marry Kate and was in the process of planning to do so soon. Apparently, it was not soon enough for either Blase or Greg. In fact, the obvious occasion for Kevin to spring the big question was Kate's upcoming advanced education degree in reading from Johns Hopkins University, which she was receiving in late May. It had gotten to the point where even Greg was thinking Kevin had perhaps gotten cold feet, and he shared his thought privately with Kevin shortly after the graduation ceremony. The engagement finally occurred a month later when Kevin threw a graduation party for Kate. Thank God she accepted!

In July 2005, Blase and Dawn made their first trip to Chautauqua. It was just about the time Blase started to have some challenges with walking. Like many middle-aged men, he had chronic back problems over the years, but this was different. In the spring, new tumors were discovered in his backbone, and they were getting precariously close to his spine. The doctors had serious concerns the tumors would reach his spine, potentially resulting in paralysis. He was starting to have more and more problems with numbness in his right leg. The hilly town of Chautauqua made things even more difficult for Blase to get around, but he was very much up to the challenge. Without question, the best way to really experience the history and spirit of Chautauqua is to walk throughout the beautiful grounds and step inside the many beautiful public buildings, historic inns, churches, and the Athenaeum Hotel, which was originally built in 1881 and was known as the first hotel in America with electricity. Although the cancer medications and the difficulty he found in walking were causing Blase to tire quickly, he was able to do quite a lot during their weekend visit, attending a concert and church services, as well as spending lots of time with the Prechtl family.

The three-story house in which Blase and Dawn were staying was owned by very close friends of the Prechtl family. After a rather long day from all the physical activity, Blase was extremely tired. His leg had become completely numb, and he couldn't walk at all, let alone get up to the second floor bedroom. After helping his dad get up the stairs and into bed, Kevin became extremely emotional. To see his dad continue to physically deteriorate and to see it happen in Chautauqua, the site of the wedding, almost a year away, caused Kevin to wonder for the first time if his dad would even be able to make it to the wedding. Just before waking the following morning, Kevin had a dream his dad had died. He immediately dressed and ran to where his mom and dad were staying, believing when he got there, he would find Blase had passed away. Fortunately, it was only a dream and Kevin thanked God.

The weeks following the Chautauqua visit continued to be very challenging for Blase. He was still walking, but with more difficulty.

The numbness in his right leg was getting progressively worse. He continued to try to do everything most people take for granted, like driving a car, playing golf, etc. We were concerned with his driving because the numbness had gotten so bad, he drove entirely with his left foot. After a while, he was forced to use a walker. His last round of golf was on February 1, 2006 when Wanda and I were visiting Dawn and Blase in Florida. I was very fortunate to have the privilege of playing what would become Blase's final round of golf. He shot a ninety-one basically playing on one foot. He took me for four bucks.

The cancer continued to spread, and Blase's ability to walk deteriorated to the point where he became paralyzed from the waist down and was relegated to a wheelchair. Being paralyzed is an incredibly difficult ordeal for anyone, and this was especially true for Blase. He was always a very active and independent person throughout his life. He loved sports and he had a daily workout routine which he followed religiously. Dealing with such a debilitating disease would have been devastating to anyone, but somehow, Blase learned how to cope and stay positive, and he adjusted to his new life in a wheelchair. It was the rest of his family and friends who were more devastated. Because of his positive attitude, many of us had maintained the belief and faith there would be a miracle and he would beat the cancer. Now it was much harder to think he would overcome both the paralysis and disease.

There were so many people who prayed for Blase throughout his illness. At that point, the question became, what do you pray for now—a cancer cure, the ability to walk, no more pain, just making it to the wedding? In my case, my prayers to God were asking to keep Blase strong mentally and spiritually, to help him get through each day, and to pray for his peace of mind. I put the rest in God's hands. Somewhere along the line, the reality of one's mortality hits you in the gut and you recognize that no one will be here forever. I am convinced our prayers were answered, because Blase continued to stay active with his mind, his spirit, and the remaining parts of his body, which still continued to work. In fact, right up until the weekend before he died, he continued to lift weights and do stretching exercises.

The back surgery took place on May 12, 2006. The motivation behind the risky surgery was simple—he wanted to dance at Kevin and Kate's wedding. Just being able to physically get to the wedding would be a major accomplishment but Blase's goal was a bit loftier. Immediately after the surgery, he went into a very intensive two-week physical rehabilitation program at Good Samaritan Hospital to try to walk again. He actually improved a bit, and we were all hoping the surgery was a success and would get him walking again, but the improvement was unfortunately short-lived.

As the wedding approached, Blase was not sure if he could physically handle the trip to Chautauqua either by car or commercial airline. In both cases, it would take a minimum of ten hours or more to get there. Given the trauma of his recent back surgery and the amazing physical effort he endured during rehab, he was seriously considering the idea that he might not be able to attend the wedding. He also did not want to be a burden for the family, and of course, he wanted all the attention to be on the bride and groom.

Through an incredible gesture from another great friend of Blase, he was able to get to and from Chautauqua in a private jet. What should have been a long, arduous journey actually became a much more manageable trip. We were able to drive the car right onto the tarmac and get Blase onto the plane quickly and easily. Thirty-five minutes later, we arrived at a small airport just outside of Chautauqua. Again, a car was waiting on the tarmac, and we were just a fifteen-minute drive away from the institution. As soon as he arrived on the grounds of Chautauqua, Blase's spirits were lifted to the point where he felt confident he was going to make it through the weekend.

The Prechtls had arranged for Dawn and Blase to stay in a house of two of their best friends who would not be attending the wedding because their son happened to be getting married in California on the same day. What's really hard to believe is that the owners added an elevator and made the house wheelchair-accessible the previous winter. Perhaps this was just a coincidence, but God does work in mysterious ways.

The words "give up" are just not in Blase's vocabulary. Somehow he willed his way to gather the strength to participate in every single event throughout the wedding weekend—from the Maryland-style crab feast on Thursday night, where he sat in a golf cart and met lots of new family and friends, to the rehearsal dinner on Friday, where he gave a beautiful speech, to the outdoor ceremony and reception, where he did dance—at least in spirit. Before leaving on Sunday, he was determined to attend Kate's parents' breakfast reception in spite of the fact he was totally exhausted and had to be carried into the house. He had decided he was not going to let his physical condition get in the way of enjoying the weekend.

Kevin's wedding day

My Brother, My Keeper

On the flight home, he was totally spent, but the adrenalin was still pumping to the point of making him giddy. I could tell how proud he was to have achieved his goal of getting to and actively participating in the wedding.

***

On Thursday, September 27, 2007, fifteen months after their wedding, Kevin and Kate came to visit Blase in the hospital. He had recently undergone a liver procedure and he had become dehydrated and was very weak. When they first arrived, Blase was sort of in and out of consciousness, but suddenly he woke up and became lucid. Kevin felt the time was right, and he mentioned an "upcoming event" to Blase which would take place in the spring of '08. Although Blase was listening, he just couldn't comprehend what Kevin was implying, so Kevin finally blurted out he and Kate would be welcoming their first child the following May. Well, the smile on Blase's face lit up the room. He was exhilarated to hear the good news. Perhaps at that point, Blase may have realized for the first time it was okay for him to think about letting go—because he knew about the circle of life.

Our family first heard about the term "circle of life" from our sister, Aggie. She has been writing "The Family Scoop" for about fifteen years. It's a monthly update on what's happening throughout our extended family: siblings, cousins, second cousins, and all their children and grandchildren, etc. Our entire family eagerly looks forward to getting our Scoop every month. It's filled with everything from birthdays to kids going off to college to job promotions, vacation trips, etc. It also includes things like births and deaths. Simply put, the circle of life occurs when someone dies and another is born. We are all eagerly looking forward to Blase and Dawn's next grandchild.

We have a very close extended family, and Aggie has been instrumental in communicating the love, commitment, and strength of

185

our family. We are very fortunate. Thanks, Ag. We love you very much for doing what you do.

Over the next few days, the awareness of the circle of life would become abundantly clear to all of us.

Excerpt from Kevin's Eulogy to Blase, October 5, 2007

No amount of public speaking classes can prepare you for a day like today. I'm honored and terrified to be speaking in front of all of you at this memorial and celebration of my father's life. The people in this room are the past, present, and future of my father. You've been with him through the hard times (losing his father, his mother, battling cancer, and losing to one of you chops on the golf course). I know you will be with us today and moving forward as we carry on the lessons we've learned from him through all these years.

As sad as today may be, the one thing that keeps me "positive," as my father would put it, is the fact that I'll be better tomorrow, and even better the next day. The fact that I have this support system in place, as do all of you, is a blessing that few share. We are grateful for that, as I am grateful for my father.

I could sit up here and recount stories of my father, the businessman. I could tell you about how he sacrificed himself unselfishly every day of my childhood to make sure we didn't "grow up eating mustard sandwiches," or that he led through example and never asked anyone to do something that he hadn't already done, and done well.

I could also write novels on my father, the philanthropist. He practiced what he learned from the Bible. He always said that if you give to those in need, the Lord will repay you tenfold. He

*truly did treat his neighbors as he would have liked to be
treated, and was indeed his brother's keeper.*

*But selfishly, I would rather tell you about my father, the father.
He was an amazing man who taught me what it meant to be a
husband, father, mentor, and friend. He taught me the game of
golf, a game that not only teaches you the importance of
competition, but also of fair play, staying positive, and focusing
on the good rather than the bad. My father came to every match
I ever had and was the captain of "my favorite foursome"
Jason, Brian, Dad, and me.*

*My father also taught me the importance of a good hug. You
can literally change a person's day with a warm embrace.
Simultaneously, he taught me of embarrassment as he would
hug me in any and every public setting. That's okay, Dad,
I wouldn't have had it any other way.*

*My father taught me how to "make it a great day." We used to
have this long winding staircase in the house where we grew
up with a mirror at the bottom of it. He would literally make us
look at ourselves in the mirror before heading off to school and
tell ourselves to "make it a great day." He taught us at an
early age that we have a choice when we wake up in the
morning; you can either choose to have a bad day, or even just
a good day, but why not MAKE it a great day? It takes a
courageous person to decide to make a great day and see to it
that it happens.*

*My father taught me of the importance of family and to hold it
above everything else. No matter what else you have going on
in your life, always remember where you came from and those
who are most important to you. For that, I will be forever
grateful.*

The story of my father hasn't been written. There is no book out there that you can read to hear these lessons as he taught them. You, however, can be the authors of this unwritten manuscript. I encourage you to continue to tell you stories of my father. There is a lesson to be learned in each and every story you have, and they should be shared. Remember him, as he will certainly remember all of you. I love you, Dad. Thank you for your unending love and support. Rest not only in peace, but in confidence that what you started will be passed down to generations to come.

Memorandum

To: All Personnel

From: Blase Cooke

Re: THOUGHT FOR THE DAY

A New Year's Prayer

May you get a clean bill of health from your dentist, your cardiologist, your urologist, your proctologist, your psychiatrist, your plumber, and the IRS.

May your hair, your teeth, your abs, and your stocks <u>not fall</u>; and may your blood pressure, your triglycerides and cholesterol, your white blood count and your mortgage rate interest <u>not rise</u>.

May what you see in the mirror delight you, and what others see in you delight them. May someone love you enough to forgive your faults, be blind to your blemishes, and tell the world of your virtues,

May you remember to say, "I love you" at least once a day to your spouse, your child, your parent, your siblings,

and may we live in a world at peace and with the awareness of God's love in every sunset, every flower's unfolding petal, every baby's smile, and every wonderful, astonishing, miraculous beat of our heart.

(Thanks to Hal Smith for this Thought for the Day.)

Chapter 11

St. Louis Church Dedication—Woodlawn, MD, April 23, 2006

"We were so moved by his faith and kindness.
His determination to fight and not
give up sends a powerful message to us (cancer) survivors."

Stephanie Stewart, November 18, 2007

Blase was a very generous person with his time, his talent, and his treasure. A great example of this was his total commitment to the Catholic Church, and in particular, to St. Louis Catholic Church, of which he was a member for over thirty years.

Blase and the family joined St. Louis Church back in 1976 when they moved to their newly built home in Howard County. The boys all attended Catholic school there, and Dawn performed various volunteer roles. Blase also took an active role in parish activities. Because of his expertise in the construction industry, he was very involved in the church's various building ventures, which included the construction of two new churches and parish ventures centers and the reconstruction of the original St. Louis Church, which was built in 1855. He served as chairman of the building committee for the church from 1980–1982, chairman of the building committee for the school from 1990–1992, and he was a member of the finance committee from 1983–1990, and the chairman of the finance committee from 1991 until his passing.

Not only did Blase get involved in these activities, he was also a major financial contributor in a number of these projects. In fact, the restoration of the old church was, some say, miraculously completed in time to bury Blase. It turns out, as good of a planner as Blase was, he had never gotten to the point of purchasing burial plots. He had decided he wanted to be buried at the site of the old church, which had a limited number of available plots, but whenever the subject came up, he would somehow put off the actual transaction itself. Just two months before he died, Dawn secretly went to Monsignor Luca, the pastor of St. Louis, and a friend of the family, and purchased the plots. The very first service in the beautifully restored old church was Blase's burial service. We could still smell the freshly painted walls.

Over the years, Blase attended daily Mass at St. Louis on a fairly regular basis. According to Monsignor Luca, he remembered many occasions when Blase would arrive to the 7:00 a.m. mass a tad late and would occasionally cause some minor disruption as he greeted other attendees who had apparently arrived on time. He was very grateful for all the goodness in his life, and daily Mass was a way he could thank God for all those blessings.

The latest and largest St. Louis Church was dedicated on April 23, 2006. It was just three weeks before Blase would undergo the back surgery to try to help him walk again. He was still using a walker, but it was getting more and more difficult, so much so that he had just recently reverted to a wheelchair at home.

Below is a direct account from Mr. J. P. Bolduc, who attended the church dedication on that beautiful spring day. Bolduc was a business associate, a member of St. Louis Church, and a friend of Blase.

It was a wonderful day. The church was filled with over 1,200 attendees. Blase and Dawn were in attendance, and so too, were Evelyn, my wife, and I. Blase and Dawn and Evelyn and I were assigned the very first pew in recognition of our contribution toward the new church.

My Brother, My Keeper

Blase was clearly in pain throughout the outdoor dedication ceremony, which had taken place earlier that day, as well as the in-church dedication, including Mass. This pain was evident when he grimaced at his every move. He was aided by a walker, which was fitted with a small seat to allow him the opportunity to rest when needed, which, of course, he would not use.

He expressed to Evelyn and me that he was scheduled for back surgery in a couple of weeks and was most optimistic that this surgery, though risky, would enable him to return to full mobility.

As the Mass progressed, it became clearly apparent that Blase was experiencing increasing difficulty in moving from a sitting to a standing position, and vice-versa. The grimace on his face, the perspiration on his forehead, and the obvious difficulty of moving up and down convinced me that I should offer to assist Blase in moving about, and what a mistake that was! There was no way he was going to submit himself to any assistance from anyone, including me. Pain or no pain, he was going to do it Blase's way—without help. He told me in very few words that he was not in need of help. He was fine, thank you!

That's the kind of stuff Blase was made of—tough, determined, courageous, and persevering, but always optimistic. How easy it would have been to accept my offer of assistance, but no, he did not need it! Nor did he want it. As we all know, the surgery later that week left him immobilized and the rest is sadly evident to all of us.

We lost a great man. He was my hero and I told him so every time I spoke or wrote him. Through all this, God has significantly strengthened his leadership team by recruiting our Blase, and we are left with a vacancy never to be filled by the likes of another.

***

193

Blase was a very charitable person, and he helped many people throughout his life, including family, friends, strangers, and especially the less fortunate of the world. He was also very grateful for the many blessings God had bestowed on him. Even though he didn't have the resources back then, I think his charitable ethic began shortly after Dad died. What he saw was a struggling widow who was trying to make ends meet. He also saw a supportive church that did not turn its back. Whether it was a break on the school tuition to attend St. Joseph Monastery or baskets of food we received during the holidays, he saw people reaching out to help others. He also witnessed his mom finding work as a clerk at a grocery store and a food server at Mt. St. Joe, doing whatever she could to help make ends meet. During his teenage years, his money from part-time jobs helped support Mom and our family. Even though he was only thirteen or fourteen years old, he inherently knew he needed to become the father figure in some form or fashion. I think he began doing exactly what his dad did—work hard. His initial charity work started at home as a result of his parents' example and grew from there.

Charity is not all about money. In fact, giving your time and talent is just as important, and perhaps even more so. In Blase's case, he was generous in every facet of giving. The story below is a great example of how Blase unknowingly helped someone by doing something as simple as participating in his child's grade school project, telling the students what he did for a living. Blase not only told the kids what he did, but more importantly, how he did it.

From Matt Wineman, grade school friend of Jason Cooke

Certainly the story that best describes your dad's impact on my life relates to a time in which he spoke to our class at St. Louis. I believe it was fourth grade, but I really can't be sure. Your dad spoke to the class about a number of things that day, but the thing that I remember most is the topic of accomplishing goals.

My Brother, My Keeper

*He said the secret to accomplishing goals was to remind
yourself every day what you are working towards. He
specifically said that the goal could be anything, whether it be
better grades or saving money to buy a bike, but the best way to
accomplish it was to write a list that included a few one-year
goals and a few five-year goals. He said to place that list in your
wallet and to work toward accomplishing your goals every day.*

*Our class did what your dad suggested as a class project, and
I recall taking his words to heart. Although since that time,
I have not always actually carried a list in my wallet, his words
have meant so much to the manner in which I view work,
accomplishments, goals, obstacles, and hardships. Most
importantly, his words have helped guide me in my efforts to
succeed in business and in life.*

*I truly treasure the opportunity to have known your dad, and
cannot imagine the countless number of lives that he has
positively affected. I consider myself blessed to be one of them.*

Matt

***

One of Blase's favorite charities is Catholic Charities of the
Archdiocese of Baltimore. Catholic Charities currently serves more
than 160,000 poor and disadvantaged people through eighty diverse
programs throughout the state of Maryland. Catholic Charities is
firmly rooted in the Gospel of Jesus to "serve the least of our
brethren," regardless of faith, race, or circumstances.

In addition to his efforts with the Catholic Charities Golf Tournament,
Blase was involved in numerous other fund raising activities over
many years. He was a board member of Catholic Charities from

195

1988–1989. He also held numerous positions for the Archdiocese of Baltimore, including:

Board Member—1990–2007
Fund Development Committee—1991–2007
Chairman, Archbishop's Lenten Appeal, Special Gifts—1994
Vice Chairman, Archbishop's Lenten Appeal—983, 1995–2007
Vice Chairman, Archbishop's Capital Campaign—1992–1998

One example of how Blase worked with Catholic Charities was on October 8, 1995, Pope John Paul II celebrated Mass before more than 50,000 worshippers at Oriole Park in Camden Yards. The altar upon which Mass was celebrated was built by Harkins Builders. During the planning phase, months before the event, Catholic Charities approached Blase and asked if Harkins would be interested in building the altar. Of course, he jumped at the opportunity, and Harkins donated the complete construction of the altar. When Harkins disassembled the altar, they took the wood from the Altar and created plaques to share with their employees, families and friends. Blase was also privileged to be invited to greet Pope John Paul II at the Mass celebrated at the Cathedral of Mary Our Queen, and he shared this awesome opportunity with our mom.

Blase and his mom greeting Pope John Paul II, 1995

As a result of the service above and numerous other charitable endeavors he undertook, Blase was honored to receive the Papal Award—Pro Ecclesia Et Pontifice Medal in 1996 and the Papal Order of Saint Gregory the Great in 2004. The Pro Ecclesia Et Pontifice Medal, also known as the Cross of Honor, is awarded for distinguished service to the church by laypeople and clergy. It is the highest medal that can be awarded to the laity by the papacy. The Order of St. Gregory is one of the five pontifical orders of knighthood in the Catholic church. The order is bestowed on Catholic men and women in recognition of their service to the church, unusual labors, support of the Holy See, and the good example set in their communities and country. Blase was extremely proud and humbled to have received these very special honors from his church.

Blase and his good friend, Bill Franey

In addition to his charitable contributions to the church, Blase also serviced his community. He was a member of the Board of Trustees of Howard County General Hospital from 1992–1999. He also served on the USO Board of Directors from 1995 to 2007. In addition, he received a public service award in 1989 and the Governor's Salute to Excellence in 1989 and 1991 from the State of Maryland.

Helping people was a part of Blase's DNA. He did it in all sorts of ways. We were on a golf trip in Florida, and we stopped for breakfast at a Waffle House. We were in a hurry to get to the golf course, so we asked our waitress if she could help expedite things. Waffle House can usually get you in and out pretty quickly anyway, but the waitress did a great job in spite of the fact she was very busy with other customers. Before anyone knew it, Blase had grabbed the check, like he often did. We were in the parking lot when the waitress came running out to thank Blase for the twenty-dollar tip he left. The meal itself probably wasn't much more than twenty dollars. Blase had realized the extra effort she made for us, and he appreciated it. She thanked him and told him that it was the largest tip she had ever received. She also mentioned that he made her day. Blase's response was that she had just made his.

Blase was a very faithful and grateful person. When he found out he had cancer, he simply accepted it. He didn't like it, but he accepted it. When he prayed to God for healing and it didn't happen, he accepted it, but he didn't stop fighting. He even tried to help others during his journey. A great example of this is a beautiful email I received from Stephanie and Jim Stewart, friends and neighbors of Blase.

Please accept Jim's and my deepest sympathies. We lost my younger brother to cancer six years ago. No one realizes the trauma until you've walked in those shoes.

We didn't realize just how many people were touched by Blase's generosity. I guess the special incident that affected us was when I was going through my cancer treatment; at the same time, Blase was having one of his many challenges, but he took the time and energy to send us well wishes, prayers, and holy water, but most of all, the courage to face this disease.

My Brother, My Keeper

*We were so moved by his faith and kindness. His determination
to fight and not give up sends a powerful message to survivors.
What an inspiration to all!*

Stephanie & Jim Stewart

Speaking of holy water, in the early fall of 2002, Blase called me and
asked if I would like to go with him to visit the Shrine of Our Lady of
Lourdes in France. He was looking for a miracle, and he thought this
would be a great place to get one. He had done some research and
determined that we could accomplish this over a weekend. We would
fly out from Washington, DC on Friday evening, October 18, arrive in
Paris early Saturday morning, and be in Lourdes before noon. We
planned on leaving Lourdes Sunday afternoon and arriving back in DC
Monday morning, October 21. That would give us almost two full
days to visit the Shrine. Blase also invited our brother, Greg, and our
brother-in-law, Jack, to go as well. He thought all four of us could use
some divine assistance and we all readily agreed. In fact, each of us
realized the divine assistance we had already received over the years,
so it would be an opportunity to express our gratitude. I am a cancer
survivor from melanoma in 1997. Greg had recently received stents to
treat blockages in his arteries, and Jack became a heart transplant
survivor in 1995. Suffice it to say, we all had much to be grateful for.

I wish I could say that our flight to Paris was great, but we did have a
few issues. First, Blase spilled salad dressing all over himself, and then
he started feeling queasy and could not find any air bags. Then the
turbulence started and lasted for quite a while. On a positive note, the
food was decent and we saw a good movie, but none of us got much
sleep. We arrived in Charles de Gaulle at 5:45 a.m. and took a bus to
Orly Airport for the connecting flight to Lourdes. The length of the
flight was only forty minutes and left on time. About ten minutes
before we were scheduled to land, the pilot came on the intercom, and

of course, was talking in French. All the people around us who understood him seemed disappointed. This was because instead of landing in Lourdes at around 10:15 a.m. as scheduled, the plane flew back to Orly for an equipment problem. Our first thought was, there goes the weekend. Fortunately, whatever was broken was fixed quickly, and we arrived in Lourdes around 12:30 p.m. We checked into the hotel, freshened up a bit, then took a five-minute walk through the little town that was just outside the Shrine of Our Lady of Lourdes.

The first apparition of Our Lady of Lourdes occurred on February 11, 1858, when Bernadette Soubirous, a fourteen-year-old peasant girl from Lourdes admitted, when questioned by her mother, that she had seen a "lady" in the cave of Massabielle. Catholics consider Bernadette a saint, and her visions have been that of the Virgin Mary. Similar appearances of the "lady" took place on seventeen more occasions that year.

Mary revealed herself as the Immaculate Conception, and asked that a chapel be built on the site of the vision. She told Bernadette to drink from a fountain in the grotto. No fountain was to be seen, but when Bernadette dug at a spot designated by the apparition, a spring began to flow. The water from this still flowing spring has shown remarkable healing power, though it contains no curative property that science can identify. Today, this same spring that was started by little Bernadette now flows at a rate of 122,400 liters per day.

Lourdes has become the most famous modern shrine of the Blessed Virgin Mary and receives more than 3.5 million visitors a year, many of them seeking miracles and cures from the holy water that flows there.

When we walked onto the grounds, we were very impressed with the size and scope of the shrine. There are three churches that were built above the grotto where all of the apparitions occurred—the Rosary Basilica, the Crypt, and the Upper Basilica. There is also the

Underground Basilica, which seats over 20,000 people and many other churches and places to pray. It was a very beautiful and peaceful site, but what was really compelling was to see so many sick and infirm people who had traveled from all parts of the world looking for a miracle from the Blessed Mother. We saw many young children with their caregivers who had obviously been stricken from birth with one terrible disease or another. It was overwhelming to witness so many sick people in one place, especially in a place like Lourdes. It was also incredibly inspiring to witness their strong faith. It didn't take long for the four of us to realize how fortunate and blessed we were. It was clear to me Blase had always accepted the fact he had cancer. He never said, why me Lord? It was also clear he believed in miracles, and he was hoping for a cure so he could lead a very long life, but at that moment on that day, we all had an epiphany—how fortunate and grateful we were to have been blessed with such bountiful and healthy lives.

Our first visit was to the Rosary Basilica, which was completed in 1889. The church can hold 2,500, although, ironically, it is not handicapped-accessible. The central dome inside the church is decorated with a mosaic of Our Lady of Lourdes. We then walked back toward the grotto and passed by the area where many people were filling bottles and jugs of holy water, which we would do ourselves the following day. We made our first visit into the grotto, which was quite emotional. The Grotto of Massabielle is where the Virgin appeared to Bernadette eighteen times, and where she said the words, "I am the Immaculate Conception."

After our visit to the grotto, we took a short walk to the baths, which are simply sixteen baths made of stone. They were constructed in 1955 and are used for worshippers to "bathe" in order to cleanse their body and wash away their sins. Before we knew it, we were nervously waiting to participate. It turned out to be a very spiritual experience, as did everything else we undertook during our weekend in Lourdes. We then went to the Crypt Church to celebrate Mass in French. The

Crypt is situated between the Upper Basilica and the Rosary Basilica and sits right on top of the Rock of Massabielle. It was built in 1866. From there, we visited the Upper Basilica, called the Immaculate Conception. The construction began in 1862 and the church opened for public worship in August 1871. It is a beautiful church with twenty-one altars and can seat one thousand people.

Perhaps the highlight of the entire weekend was the torchlight procession, which took place at 8:45 p.m. on Saturday evening. We had a pleasant dinner at the hotel, then walked back to the shrine and were stunned when we saw all the people. The procession began at the grotto with everyone lighting their candles and then singing the "Salve Regina." We walked around the esplanade saying the rosary in five different languages and singing of the "Ave Maria." What a beautiful ending to an inspiring day.

The next morning, Blase and I overslept and didn't wake up until 9:00 a.m. We were a bit late for an English-speaking Mass, which took place in one of the chapels at the shrine. We then went to an international Mass in the underground basilica of Saint Pius X, another amazing experience. After Mass, we did what all the tourists do when they come to Lourdes—we drank the holy water of Lourdes and we proceeded to fill up as many bottles as we could carry back on the plane. Breakfast followed, the highlight of which was Jack ordering an ice cream sundae. After dropping our holy water off at the hotel, we visited the grotto and Crypt Church for a second time. We also lit some very large candles and made our petitions to the Virgin Mary to heal Blase. Afterward, we decided to make the Stations of the Cross, which was actually a fairly long hike up, over, and back down a steep hill, with each station separated by approximately one block. Perhaps it was the ice cream, but shortly into our walk, Jack was having some difficulty with the steep hill. We were discussing whether we should continue or have Jack return to the entrance where we would meet up later. Then we saw a little old lady, probably in her eighties, walk right by us, continuing up the hill. That was all the motivation Jack needed. I'm happy to report that Jack, the little old lady, and the rest of us survived the stations and made it back down the hill in good shape.

We got back just in time for the start of the blessed sacrament procession, which, along with the torchlight procession, are the two daily processions that take place every day at the shrine. This procession ended with a benediction at the Rosary Basilica. Our flight home, although long, was uneventful.

Blase at the Rosary Basilica in Lourdes, France

In retrospect, although we went to Lourdes with a purpose, and we prayed for a miracle for Blase, we realized how many blessings we had already received and how fortunate we were in so many ways. Blase had already accepted his situation with cancer. He wasn't bitter, and he certainly didn't feel sorry for himself. He also didn't get the miracle he was hoping for. However, I believe, as time went on and things got worse, he somehow garnered the strength to handle his suffering. Perhaps God gave him this ultimate challenge and maybe his real purpose in this life was to be a living example of how to handle this kind of suffering and adversity. Perhaps that is the miracle he received from his trip to Lourdes.

Memorandum

To: All Personnel

From: Blase Cooke

Re: THOUGHT FOR THE DAY

The Interview

I dreamed I had an interview with God.

"So, you would like to interview me?" God asked.

"If You have the time," I said.

God smiled, "My time is eternity. What questions do you have in mind to ask me?"

"What surprises You most about humankind?"

God answered, "That they get bored with childhood—they rush to grow up and then long to be children again."

"That they lose their health to make money and lose their money to restore their health."

"That by anxiously thinking about the future, they forget the present, such that they live in neither the present nor the future."

"That they live as if they never die and they die as if they had never lived."

God's hands took mine and we were silent for a while and then I asked, "As a parent, what are some of life's lessons You want your children to learn?"

God replied with a smile:

"To learn that they cannot make anyone love them. What they can do is to let themselves be loved."

"To learn that what is most valuable is not what they have in their lives, but who they have in their lives."

"To learn that it is not good to compare themselves to others."

"To learn that a rich person is not the one who has the most, but is one who needs the least."

"To learn that it only takes a few seconds to open profound wounds in persons one loves and that it may take many years to heal them."

"To learn to forgive by practicing forgiveness."

"To learn that there are persons who love them dearly, but simply do not know how to express or show their feelings."

"To learn that money can't buy everything, especially happiness."

"To learn that two people can look at the same thing and see it very differently."

"To learn that it is not always enough that they be forgiven by others, but they must also forgive themselves."

"And to learn that I am here – always."

Author: Unknown

Thanks to Edwards Holliday for this thought.

Chapter 12   *My Brother, My Keeper*

The Funeral, St. Louis Catholic Church—
Clarksville, Maryland, October 5, 2007

Well done, good and faithful servant.

Matthew 25:21

These words from the Gospel of St. Matthew appeared on the front page of the program at Blase's funeral. Many people mentioned it was a perfect description of how he led all aspects of his life and how he will be remembered. More than one thousand people showed up for the funeral and it was a beautiful and well-deserved tribute to Blase.

Just a few days before Blase passed away, he was back in the hospital. He had become dehydrated from what ended up being his final attempt at prolonging his life. The doctors had concluded the tumors in his liver had become so pervasive it would eventually result in liver failure and kill him, so he decided to undertake the first of two invasive procedures that would occur over a four-week period to reduce the tumors in order to hopefully extend his a life a few more months. He got through the first procedure on September 19 and returned home, but a week later, ended up back in the hospital. He never got the opportunity to do the second procedure.

On Sunday, September 30, he was back home, where he would spend his final two days. Two nights before, while in the hospital, he had two separate choking incidents where Dawn thought he almost died. She was afraid to leave him, so she spent the night in the hospital. When Joey arrived the next day, Dawn was totally exhausted, so Joey stayed in the hospital with Blase the following night. That evening, Blase had a hallucination that there was a fire in the hospital. Joey tried to comfort him, but he told her to get out and save herself. Then he remembered there were wheels on the hospital bed and that perhaps Joey could roll him out of the room. I am no expert on dream interpretation, but it seems pretty apparent to me that Blase was still not ready to give it up. He was still trying to prolong his life. Throughout the remainder of that night, he had other hallucinations, but none that Joey could understand.

Like every day for the past six and a half years, he woke up on Monday, ready to tackle the challenges of another day. He had regained a little strength, but was still quite weak. For the past year, since becoming paralyzed, every morning Dawn, Joelyn, or his nurse, Cindy, were there to help bathe, massage and dress him. He would then brush his teeth, shave, and comb his hair. I remember being there a few times while he was getting ready to start his day, and he would tell me that just performing those tasks would exhaust him. On this particular Monday, the day before he died, he was in and out of consciousness, although he did attempt to go through his Harkins folder. Sitting in his wheelchair, he would pick up a document or piece of mail and sort of look at it, then throw it on the floor. He was still trying, but he was just going through the motions. Dawn did help him get through the beautiful letter from Joani acknowledging her twenty-five-year anniversary with Harkins, and he was very touched by her kind words. And even on his last day, he did his daily exercise routine with Joey.

The next morning, October 2, was our mom's birthday. She died on December 27, 1997, at the age of eighty-two. October 2 also happens to be the Feast of the Guardian Angels. Coincidence? I don't think so. When Blase awoke that morning around 7:00 a.m., he was very thirsty and tried to drink some water. He started choking. Dawn was able to lift his head up and the choking stopped. Blase still seemed uncomfortable, indicating he couldn't swallow and was having difficulty breathing. Then he shocked Dawn when he suggested that perhaps he should go back to the hospital. Just the day before, he had told Dawn he never wanted to go back to the hospital again. Clearly, Dawn was concerned. She went upstairs to get Joelynn and they suggested he take a pain pill to help him relax. They began stroking his cold hands. They could always tell when Blase was stressed because his hands would be cold. Cold hands were an inherited trait from our mom, a very anxious person by nature. She used to say, "If you have cold hands, you have a warm heart." They continued to rub Blase's hands and asked him to relax. His reply, which were the last words he would ever say, were: "Honey, I'll try." Then Dawn and Joelyn went into the family room to discuss what they should do. Dawn thought that perhaps it was finally time to consider some type of in-home hospice care. They were only gone a few minutes when they heard a slight cough from the monitor in Blase's room. Then it was quiet. A couple of minutes passed, and Joey thought it was perhaps too quiet. She decided to go back to check on him and, that quickly, Blase was gone. Joey then did the hardest thing she had ever done in her life—she put her head on his chest to try to hear a heartbeat and there was none. Since they had not heard anything unusual, they believe he passed peacefully. After what he went through, if anyone deserved a quiet death it was Blasé, and we were so thankful to God for that. When Dawn came back into the room, she stroked his face and grasped his hands—they were warm.

Jack and Jul, who lived just down the road, were the first to arrive. Jul grasped Blase's hand and rubbed his arm and felt warmth. Then she hugged his body and felt the warmth again. She had always thought that when a person dies, the body gets cold. Blase's body was at the house for more than four hours before he was taken, and when we said our last goodbye, his body was still warm.

***

Wanda called me in my office around 8:40 a.m. She didn't know any other way to put it other than to say that Blase had just died. You would think having a prolonged illness like cancer would better prepare you to receive this kind of news. Although I had shed many tears over the years knowing he was eventually going to die, I was still shocked when it happened.

For whatever reason, I didn't cry until I returned home to pick up Wanda to drive back to Blase's house, and even then I didn't cry very much. Perhaps I was still in shock. The one-hour drive from our home in northern Virginia to Blase's home took longer than usual. Normally, I am always in a hurry—it's my nature—but on this particular morning, I suspect I was trying to put off the inevitable. When we arrived, Dawn and Jason greeted us at the door. We proceeded into the master bedroom to find Blase surrounded by my sisters, Ag, and Jul, Jul's husband, Jack, and my brother, Greg, with his wife, Bonnie. Brian, Kevin, and the boys' spouses, Alexis, Kerri, and Kate, were there too, as well as Joani. Father Mike Murphy was there as well, providing support throughout the day, just as he had been throughout Blase's illness.

I don't know how long I cried. I remember I wanted to stop, but I couldn't. We all sat around his bed, touching him, stroking his head. We were relieved his physical suffering was over, and we knew he was in a better place, but it still hurt that he was gone. Blase was the rock of our family, the go-to guy, the mentor, and the "leader of our band." The good news is we had so many great and happy memories, so many great stories, and most importantly, his spirit, which we knew would never die.

After the crying subsided, some of those stories and memories of Blase began to emerge, and we realized his spirit was, in fact, alive and well. At this point, Jul decided to share a very special story with us for the first time. About a week prior to Blase's passing, she visited with a psychic. Jul is a believer in life after death, but she is not what I would call a big believer in paranormal phenomena, nor does she regularly meet with psychics. She had never met this man before. As soon as they sat down, he immediately started to talk about the spirits of our mom and dad. He said that our brother was very sick and that our mom would not go into the "light" and that our dad had come out of the "light" to be with her. He told Jul that she needed to tell Mom to go into the "light." At that time, she thought Blase had at least another six months to live, but she started praying and asking Mom to go into the "light" and wait for Blase to join her and our dad. Blase died on her birth date.

Blase, too, was not a big believer in paranormal phenomena, although he very often had acupuncture therapy and also had a friend who performed reiki therapy. In reiki, the therapist places his or her hands in a series of very light touches at various positions on the client's body. Reiki is not a massage, but a channeling of life force energy to the recipient. People who receive treatments like acupuncture and reiki often claim to have been helped with pain relief, stress, surgery recovery, and chemotherapy treatments. There have been a number of scientific studies which have shown benefits for these energy healing practices.

On the morning Blase died, one of his therapists had a dream that Blase came to her and told her he wanted to let go, but was concerned it may not be the right thing to do. Her response was that it was okay, and after six and a half years of doing everything he could to extend his life, Blase finally let go.

Five eulogies were offered at his funeral that October morning, in addition to a wonderful homily delivered by Monsignor Luca. At the beginning of the service, prior to the start of the Mass, Bill Franey and I delivered our eulogies.

During Monsignor Luca's sermon, he observed how Blase's given name of Joseph Peter was a great reflection on the type of man he had become. St. Joseph was a carpenter and a great family man. He was also very humble and hard-working. Blase carried all these traits. He also compared Blase to St. Peter, who became the leader of the Apostles and was the first head of the entire Catholic Church. Blase clearly was a leader in all aspects of his life and certainly was the rock of our family. He also talked about Blase's suffering throughout his cancer ordeal and how well he handled it. He provided one example in particular that touched him, the day of the dedication of the new church in which we were sitting. He talked about how Blase could hardly walk, yet he somehow made it through the two-hour service. Monsignor Luca pointed to where Blase was sitting that day and he recalled the anguish on his face as he struggled throughout the service.

There was another man at the funeral that day who struggled to stand up as well, but he did. Retired Archbishop William Borders, who, at almost ninety-four years old, does not get around much these days, and when he does, he needs a walker and some assistance. Without question, the former Archbishop of Baltimore was one of Blase's real heroes. The Archbishop was sitting on the altar during the funeral service. After the gospel and the beautiful sermon from Monsignor Luca, it was time to stand for the offertory prayers. We all watched as the Archbishop valiantly, and with no help, struggled to stand. He did it on his own, and I'm sure he did it as a tribute to Blase. It was a very poignant moment, and one I will never forget.

Immediately following the communion service, Jason, Brian, and Kevin delivered their eulogies. When we reviewed our original drafts two days earlier, I found it amazing that there was practically no overlap in what all of us were saying. I know Blase was very proud of his boys that day.

Blase was buried just up the road in a small graveyard at the location of the original St. Louis Church. It was a private service with just his immediate family and his siblings because it would have been impossible to accommodate the hundreds of people who surely would have attended. Following the service, there was a luncheon at Cattail Creek Country Club.

I'm sure Blase enjoyed the service. The songs and hymns, which were some of his favorites, were beautifully delivered, and he would have been humbled by all the wonderful things said about him. I am comforted because I believe he was there with us in spirit, and he will continue to be a positive and comforting influence on all those he touched.

Well done, good and faithful servant.

My excerpted eulogy to Blase—October 5, 2007

Dawn, Jason, Brian, and Kevin, thanks for giving me the honor of offering this eulogy to celebrate Blase's life, and on behalf of our entire family, thanks to everyone here for your kind words, your support, and especially your prayers for Blase and the family over the past six-and-one-half years.

We thought we would honor Blase today by describing five of his best qualities: his positive attitude, his work ethic, his competitive nature, his gratefulness, and his passion for living. My biggest challenge, of course, was limiting myself to just five qualities.

Let's start with Blase's positive attitude. Please raise your hand if you have ever had a discussion or received a comment, email, book, audio tape, or lecture from Blase on having a positive attitude. I'm not really sure when it all started, but sometime in his late twenties, Blase got hooked on the power of positive thinking, and it became a focal point throughout his life. He read and listened to the experts in the field like Earl

Nightingale, Dennis Whately, Zig Ziglar, Dr. Norman Vincent Peale, and Og Mandino, to name a few. He truly believed in the power of positive thinking, and he believed much of his success in life was a direct result of maintaining a positive attitude, and more importantly, rather than protecting his secret for success, he willingly shared it with anyone who would listen. He also learned that no matter how bad things were going, he should always maintain a positive attitude, so whenever someone asked him how he was doing, no matter how he felt or what challenges he was facing on any given day, he always responded with the word TERRIFIC!

His positive attitude led to developing annual written goals and objectives to include personal, family, and business goals. These goals were both tactical and strategic, short-term and long-term, and he would read them constantly to make sure he was on track. He would strongly encourage Jason, Brian, and Kevin to write down their goals and build a positive game plan as well, and we know they listened because it's hard to find three finer young men than Jason, Brian, and Kevin. Blase's proudest accomplishment in life is his family, and he and Dawn have so much to be proud of.

The next quality is his work ethic. Simply put, Blase worked hard at everything. Our dad died of a massive heart attack in 1959 at the age of forty-three. Blase was twelve years old. We didn't really know a lot about our dad for two reasons: we were all very young, and he worked a lot. Like many dads in our generation, he fought in World War II, and when he finally returned from the War in his early thirties, he had a lot of catching up to do. Mom and Dad were married in 1946, had five children in ten years, and like many families in those days, Dad worked two jobs to support his family. After Dad died, the one thing we inherently knew then and were able to better appreciate as we got older, was that our dad probably worked himself to death in raising his family. That's how important family was to him. After Dad died, Mom's income was basically from the government, but she, too, showed her work ethic by taking jobs at the High's Milk Store and the Mt. St. Joe cafeteria in order to make ends meet, so our mom was also very instrumental in helping Blase understand the importance of discipline and hard work.

In his teenage years, Blase had a newspaper route, worked in a subshop, caddied on weekends at Turf Valley, and worked construction. Most of the money he earned went to help with family living expenses. When Blase was drafted into the army in 1966, he further demonstrated his ethic of hard work and discipline by doing well in basic and advanced training and earned the right to be selected to train in the military police. He graduated from MP school near the top of his class as well. After his discharge, he joined Harkins Builders, where he became a true American success story—rising from a laborer to the CEO, through discipline, hard work, and perseverance. He also found time to earn a degree from the University of Baltimore, coach his kids in sports, and play softball and volleyball for the Sundancers, and he also loved to dance, but we will get to that later. Discipline and hard work was Blase's mantra. He may not have been the smartest guy or the most athletic guy, and was perhaps not the most handsome guy (although Dawn would disagree), but there was no one who was more disciplined, better prepared, or more determined than Blase, whether it was a putt to win a match on the eighteenth hole or a multimillion-dollar contract negotiation.

Next we will talk about competition. Yes, in case you didn't know it, Blase was a fierce competitor. He just loved to win, but more importantly, he loved to compete. In his younger years, it was neighborhood baseball and football on Monastery Avenue.

As a teenager in Uplands, he played a lot of cards and basketball, and hung out at Knocko's Pool Hall on Liberty Heights Avenue. Almost anything and everything became a competition. Let me share a few other competitive events that Blase loved:

Who could get the closest parking spot?

Who could get out of a parking lot faster?

The annual SuperStars Competition, which included pool, tennis, racquetball, darts, ping-pong, horse, and Ms. Pac Man. Coincidentally, Blase just happened to be pretty good in all of these events, or he thought he was. When he realized he wasn't very good in darts, the dartboard somehow disappeared from his basement the following year.

Then there was horseshoes and diving contests at the Young family reunions.

The Family Olympics – Blase was at his best during the jump rope and orange pass events.

And all the family events during vacations at the beach like home run derby, paddle ball, and the cherry pit spitting contest.

Yes, Blase loved to compete. He even competed on the dance floor. For a guy who was tone deaf and had no rhythm whatsoever, he was quite a dancer. He was the only guy we ever saw do a triple spin in a cha-cha, and his electric slide and macarena moves were, let's say, unique. Blase also loved to sing and compete in karaoke contests. By the way, all of our friends and family were so happy that somebody invented karaokee because now he finally knew some of the words. One of his

My Brother, My Keeper

favorite songs was "I Hope You Dance," by LeeAnn Womack.
I want to share with you his favorite verse from that song.

I hope you never lose your sense of wonder

You get your fill to eat, but always keep that hunger

May you never take one single breath for granted

God forbid love ever leave you empty-handed

I hope you still feel small when you stand by the ocean

Whenever one door closes, I hope one more opens

Promise me you'll give fate a fighting chance

And when you get the choice to sit it out or dance

I hope you dance

Whether it was a gin game, World Series of Poker, golf, or a
cha-cha with Dawn, it was always a competition, always fun,
and always fair. Everyone loved to compete with Blase.

Perhaps Blase's strongest quality was gratefulness. Blase was
incredibly grateful for all the wonderful blessings he received
throughout his life. Earlier, I talked about the sudden death of
our dad. Over the years, Blase and I talked often about our dad
and all the things he never got to see during his short lifetime:

> *He never saw his children graduate from grade school*
> *Or play sports in high school*
> *Or get married.*
> *He never saw his grandchildren.*

*I know Blase was so grateful and so appreciative of all of the
things our dad was unable to see that he never took anything
for granted, especially when it came to family.*

*When he got the initial news about his cancer, he did what he
had been doing all of his adult life—he developed a plan on how
he was going to win. Although this vicious disease took a major
toll on him in the ultimate physical way, cancer did not win. And
of course, like Blase has done for many of us over most of his
life—he taught us how to handle this particular adversity in a
very special way. He couldn't have accomplished his plan
without the love, kindness, and prayers from all of you—his
family and friends. Believe me, he was both humble and grateful
for every thought, every call, every note, and every prayer.*

*And he was most grateful for the amazing support he received
from both the people that have been the closest to him
throughout his life and those special people he met as a result of
his illness. People like Cindy, who has provided full-time in-home
care and love for the past eighteen months, and all the other
nurses and doctors both in Maryland and Florida who cared for
Blase. Dawn, you truly exemplified your vows from thirty-nine
years of marriage by accepting Blase in sickness and in health.
Joelyn, you became Blase's guardian angel with your unyielding
care and love. Somehow, you were able to respond to his needs
before he even asked. You were truly a gift from God when Blase
and Dawn needed it the most. Jason and Alexis, Brian and Kerri,
Kevin and Kate, and your beautiful children, you helped Blase
through this ordeal in ways you don't even know. He is forever
grateful to all of you for your love and support. I know his
happiest times were when you guys were around him.*

*Finally, I want to talk about Blase and his passion for living.
Throughout his life, he consistently gave his time, his talent,*

and his treasure. He gave it freely, with no strings attached and not looking for or expecting anything in return. He gave to his God, his family, his friends, Harkins employees, and strangers. This beautiful church we are sitting in today is a great example of his giving. The generous donations that will be received in his honor will be given to My Brother's Keeper to help sustain those less fortunate people living in Irvington area.

Blase was also passionate about giving advice on almost any topic, including politics, religion, Tiger Woods, and occasionally, he would have a word or two to say about Bill and Hillary. Although Blase was not an email kind of a guy, through the help of Joani, he was able to share things he was passionate about to so many of his family, friends, and colleagues, including his inspirational Thought for the Day emails. I know we will all miss those emails.

As busy as Blase was with his business, family, charitable, and other activities, he always somehow found the time to have that one-on-one conversation with anyone to give whatever help or assistance he or she needed. He was a giver in every sense of the word.

Blase fought as hard as he possibly could to beat this terrible disease. He made a decision years ago that he would take quantity over quality in order to extend his time as long as possible in the hope of finding either a cure or a miracle. I believe Blase finally decided he had exhausted every option and he put himself in God's hands. I know he felt Mom's desire to bring him to his eternal home, and I'm sure he knew, as he did in every phase of his life, that he did everything in his power to win. His suffering showed us all how to deal with adversity. Yes, Blase definitely had a passion for living.

Phil Cooke

Over the past couple of days, so many people have told us that if there was anyone who deserved a fast track to Heaven, it was Blase. So let me tell you how I believe Blase spent his first day in Heaven. The first thing he did was take a long walk. Then he had his favorite breakfast with his mom and dad, creamed chip beef, and perhaps a bran muffin. Since he had not been able to play golf for a while, I'm sure he was anxious to get out and play—with Mike and Billy and Pete, and many other friends and family who would like to get some of their money back. After golf, I'm guessing he checked in with whoever was in charge of fundraising to see what he could do to help, then an after-dinner pitch game with our dad and his aunts and uncles, who taught him how to play cards when he was six years old. Finally, before turning in for a restful night, I'm sure he is returning all the prayers he received from us to show his gratitude.

Here is the best news of all for those he left behind. Although we have lost a true hero, a role model, and an all-around great guy, we didn't lose his spirit, his inspiration, all of our wonderful memories of him, and best of all, we now have access to a guardian angel, who will continue to guide us and inspire us, because we will never forget Blase's spirit.

Memorandum

A DREAM

One night I had a dream,

I dreamed I was walking along the beach with the Lord,
and across the sky flashed scenes from my life.

For each scene, I noticed two sets of footprints in the sand;
one belonged to me, the other to the Lord.

When the last scene of my life flashed before me,
I looked back at the footprints in the sand.

I noticed that many times along the path of life,
there was only one set of footprints.

I noticed that it happened at the very lowest and saddest times
in my life.

This really bothered me and I questioned the Lord about it.

"Lord, You said that once I decided to follow You, You would walk
with me all the way."

"But I have noticed that during the most troublesome times in my life, there is only one set of footprints."

"I don't understand why in times I need You most, You would leave me."

The Lord replied, "My precious, precious child, I love you and I would never, never leave you during your time of trial and suffering."

"When you see only one set of footprints –

It was then that I carried you."

Anonymous

Thought courtesy of Terry Cavanaugh, Chubb Group of Insurance Companies

Chapter 13

Moving On . . .

If there is anything in this life we know with absolute certainty, it's that we are all going to die. We can't escape it. Nobody can.

Like most of us, Blase hated hospitals. Over the course of his cancer journey, he made a number of decisions regarding his treatment, which required numerous tests, procedures, and surgeries resulting in many hospital visits, some of which requiring lengthy stays. This is not to mention the additional pain he had to endure in undertaking these procedures, but neither his dislike for hospitals nor the pain he endured was going to stop him from trying to find a way to stay alive for as long as possible. At some point early on in his fight with this insipid disease, and after it was apparent the cancer had spread, he made a critical decision—he would accept quantity over quality in order to extend his life for as long as possible. This is what drove him.

About three years into Blase's cancer journey, our friend, Laura, gave me a book entitled, *Final Gifts*, by Maggie Callanan and Patricia Kelley. The book is about understanding the needs of terminally ill people. Maggie and Patricia, two hospice nurses, share their intimate experiences with their patients as they move through the process of dying. As mentioned in the book, Dr. Kubler-Ross discovers a number of specific stages most people go through during the dying process which include denial, anger, bargaining, depression, and finally, acceptance. The book was a tremendous help for me, and I would strongly recommend it to anyone who has a family member going through a terminal illness. I made the assumption that Blase would eventually end up in some type of hospice care, but I was wrong. Basically, in order to qualify for hospice care, a patient cannot be on any type of treatment other than for pain management. I have read that the

223

approach to hospice care is to improve the quality of life for patients and their families facing the problems associated with life-threatening illness through pain management to relieve physical pain, as well as providing psychological and spiritual support to the patient and family.

In Blase's case, he had already made the decision that he would exhaust every means possible to beat the disease. In fact, he disliked taking pain medication because he knew it could be addictive and he wanted to make sure he would not become dependent, so when his cure came, he would be able to get back to normal more quickly. Blase was very fortunate to have excellent hospice-like assistance at home to help with both his cancer and his paralysis and was very grateful to have such wonderful support, care, and love. In his mind, he believed that succumbing to hospice would be tantamount to giving up. That, of course, was against everything he stood for and counter to how he led his life.

After reading *Final Gifts*, I began to look for indications of when he would move into or out of the various stages of dying in hope that I could respond better to his needs at a given point in time. Because of his lifelong practice of maintaining a positive attitude, I believe he was primarily in the denial stage of the process for a very long time, perhaps right up until he actually died. It wasn't as if Blase was naïve. He knew he had cancer and that it had spread, but he was firmly convinced the chemotherapy or radiation would eventually eliminate the tumors from his system. And if conventional healing didn't work, he believed he would experience a miraculous healing. In his mind, having a positive outlook would help with a cure, whereas dwelling on dying from cancer would only hasten the outcome.

With regard to anger, if he was in this stage at all, it would have been only for very brief periods. One of the things Blase expressed early on was that cancer is not unlike a card game. Sometimes you are dealt a good hand, and sometimes you get a bad hand, but whatever hand you get, you still have to play the game. Angry people may ask God, "Why me?" while others may respond, "Why not me?" I think Blase learned a lot about himself when he took the trip to Lourdes. Perhaps that's what gave him the strength to accept the cards he had been dealt.

There was definitely bargaining going on throughout Blase's battle with cancer. He looked for any and all potential alternatives, both physically and spiritually, to rid himself from the disease. He was in constant communication with his doctors, providing them anything he thought might be useful, from research reports on new cancer therapies to all-natural diets and everything in between. Even if his last chemo embolization procedure on his liver had been successful, it would have probably given him just a few more months to live.

To say Blase went through periods of depression would be both unfair and inaccurate. Clearly, he had some occasional down times, but they didn't last very long. Throughout the entire process in dealing with his cancer and paralysis, he continued to work, read, play golf (until he could no longer walk), lift weights, ride a bike, and do his stretching exercises, and no matter how bad he felt, whenever he saw one of his kids or grandkids, he would immediately light up.

Because Blase was so focused on living, accepting the notion he was ready to let go and die, I believe, was extremely difficult for him. It wasn't so much that he was afraid of dying, but more so the fact he would miss the joy of living. I believe acceptance finally did come for Blase just a few minutes before he died on October 2, 2007, and I am totally convinced our mom in Heaven had a lot to do with helping him let go and come home to his final resting place.

What kind of lessons can we take from this experience that might help us in our journey through life? I'm not recommending for even a minute that everyone should take quantity over quality or vice-versa. The point here is most of us have choices. Unfortunately, in our society today, many times our choices can be limited based upon things like the type of medical insurance we have, how much money we have, where we live, what type of medical care may be available to us, among other things. Blase was very fortunate in that he was able to explore many options because he had financial resources and access to the best medical treatment available. Even though we are the richest country in the world, most people don't have that luxury.

I believe there are a number of life lessons we can learn from Blase with regard to how he handled his challenges with cancer, and more fundamentally, how he lived his life. Simply put, he worked hard, he was a good person, and he was very grateful to God for everything he accomplished. Blase was able to achieve a tremendous amount of success and have a positive influence on many people. He believed it had a lot to do with being honest with yourself and maintaining balance in your life. Our cousin, Patrick, who is the youngest son of our Aunt Rita and Uncle Bill, recalls a summer evening in the early eighties when he asked Blase a question about success.

Pat Walsh, Blase's cousin

One night, many years ago, during a cousin's party, while the two of us, just Blase and I, were sitting by the pool at his beautiful home in Woodmark, I had an opportunity to ask Blase a question related to how he had accomplished so much at such a young age. The house in Woodmark, by the way, was to many of us the most magnificent house any of us had seen, and we all realized that Blase was very successful, although I don't think many of us realized how successful, especially related to his charitable works.

Blase's answer to my question was that he considered his life like a table with four legs, with each leg representing a very important part of his life. Blase's four legs represented church, family, business, and personal time. Blase said that if you were spending too much time on one area of your life, the leg representing that part of your life would be too long and your table would be unbalanced. As well, Blase said if you were not spending enough time in another area, the leg would be too short and your life would be unbalanced as well.

Simple, but profound!

The most important part, however, of the example that Blase explained that night was that Blase said if you were honest with yourself, you would know if your life was in balance or out of balance, and when you were truly honest with yourself and realized your table was unbalanced, the most important thing was you made adjustments to get your life in balance.

Sounds simple, is profound, but can be very difficult to do!

This is a small example of Blase's thinking from many years ago on how important God and charity, Dawn and his sons, his brothers and sisters, his family, his friends, the Harkins organization and his golfing buddies were to him, and yet he used a simple way to explain how he kept track of how he was doing in his life with regard to his important priorities.

We can all use the example as a way to see how we are doing in our lives and to make sure we don't lose sight of what is important to each of us and our families.

This story is a great example of how a life well-balanced can be a life well lived and truly a "Lesson on Life from Blase."

Thanks, Blase, for continuing to bless us with these opportunities to learn from you.

I believe Patrick's memory of Blase provides the basic foundation for helping anyone lead a better life. Regardless of where we are in our lives today, if we could all make a few changes, we could make life better for ourselves, for family, friends, and coworkers around us, and even for people we don't know. Every day, we wake up to face new challenges, some good and some bad. One day, many years ago, a twelve-year-old child woke up and realized his dad was gone forever. In the fall of 2007, a wife and her three sons woke up and realized that their family would never be the same again. It certainly is easier for all of us to be better people when things are going well. The real test is how we handle adversity. Of all the good things Blase did in his life, and he did a lot, I believe his true legacy was how he handled the hardest part of his life, his experience with cancer. Ironically, he handled the hard part the exact same way he handled his successes in life. He continued to strive to keep his table in balance.

***

Blase made a positive and profound impact on many people throughout all walks of life. Below are some of the more significant qualities, attitudes, and habits he tried to project in order to help him maintain balance and lead a good life. Perhaps we all may want to consider some of these as we continue our journey.

Positive attitude

There are lots of motivational resources available to help develop and maintain a positive attitude, including books, seminars, tapes, and CDs. Blase availed himself to all of them. He also shared them with family, friends, and coworkers. Included in this book is a recommended list on some of his favorite motivational speakers and authors. One of his favorite ways of ensuring a positive outlook was no matter how bad he felt or no matter how bad his day might be going, whenever anyone greeted him and asked how he was doing, he always responded, "TERRIFIC," which he learned from Ed Foreman, one of his first and favorite motivational speakers.

Work hard

Blase had a very impressive work ethic and he worked hard in every aspect of his life. He focused on taking both the responsibility and action to solve problems rather than put them off for another day. He liked to get things done and he encouraged others to do the same. Hard work never hurt anyone.

Hug the ones you love

Most people like to be hugged, and Blase was one of the best huggers ever. It's a great way to show your affection. In today's world, we could all use a good hug now and then. Remember, if you give people a hug, you will be hugged in return. It's a win-win for everyone.

Read to exercise and improve your mind

Blase liked to read and he read all types of books, both fiction and nonfiction. He also read the daily paper and the *Wall Street Journal* every day. Even if he were away on a trip for a week or more, when he returned, he would make sure he went through the stack of daily papers. He would typically read two or three books simultaneously. He liked authors ranging from James Michner to David Balducci. He enjoyed reading biographies about successful people to better understand what qualities made them successful so he could then try to incorporate those qualities into his life. And when he did read a book he thought helped him, he would purchase a few dozen and send them out to family, friends, and coworkers, depending upon the type of book. He started this practice in the late nineties. Perhaps that's where Oprah got the idea for her book club.

Create goals every year, write them down, and read them often

Everyone should have goals, and if you write them down and look at them often, you will have a much higher probability of reaching your goals. You should consider setting personal, professional, and family goals. You should also have both short-term (daily, weekly, monthly, and annual) and long-term (three-year, five-year and lifetime) goals. And be sure to make very explicit goals. The more explicit you make a goal, the better chance you have of attaining it. Below is an example of an annual goal plan. Blase developed a written plan every year very similar to the one outlined below. Note this includes personal, professional, and family goals.

XXXX Goals and Objectives—January 1, XXXX

Daily

1) I will exercise every day, cardio, sit-ups, push-ups, and stretching. Weigh in every day with a goal of never being higher than 182 pounds.

2) I will read daily affirmations and listen to self-improvement programs.

3) I will thank God for everything He has given us.

4) I will control my emotions and be patient with everyone.

5) I will maintain a positive attitude and instill positive values.

6) I will think about what I eat and maintain a low-cholesterol, high-fiber diet.

Weekly

1) I will get acupuncture and massage treatments.

2) I will attend Mass every week and at least one day during the week.

3) I will attend the boys' sporting events as often as possible.

4) I will try to play or practice golf one or two times per week and improve my handicap to a six.

5) I will spend quality time with the family.

Monthly

1) I will read at least one book per month—Michner, self-improvement, business, etc.

2) Golf trips to Palm Springs, Myrtle Beach, Banyon Dunes, and Ocean City.

3) Family trips to Aspen, Ocean City, and Nantucket.

Annual

1) I will exceed the corporate revenue and profit targets by at least 25%.

2) I will actively participate in at least two professional organizations.

3) I will read and practice *the Greatest Salesman in the World.*

4) I will attend and bring others to at least one self-improvement event.

5) I will help others to reach their potential and be successful.

6) I will schedule an annual physical.

7) Maintain charitable and political involvement.

8) Successfully chair Catholic Charities Golf Classic and Archbishop Lenten Appeal.

Lifetime

1) I will lead a good religious life and I will be charitable to others.

2) I will stay fit and healthy through regular exercise, sports, and a good diet.

3) I will be a good husband, father, grandfather, and friend.

4) I will set an example of positive thinking and a positive attitude.

5) I will play at Augusta.

6) I will own a spectacular home on the water.

7) I will be a great philanthropist.

8) I will achieve peace of mind.

Accomplish what is important

In today's fast-paced twenty-four-seven world, we are constantly bombarded with information, emails, voice mails, meetings, and many other potential distractions which, if we are not careful, can take up most, if not all of our day. Some call it information overload. Blase developed a habit of creating a daily list of priorities. At the end of a day, he would make a note of the most important things he needed to accomplish the following day. On some days, he may have had just one goal to accomplish; on other days, he may have had ten priorities. Of course, he didn't always accomplish every task, but having a list and focusing on that list surely increased the probability.

Accept the cards you are dealt

It's easy to be happy and content when things are going well. The real test comes when adversity strikes—losing your job, divorce, an illness, death in the family, etc.

Be honest with yourself

This sounds easy, but hard to do because your ego will get in the way. If you are honest with yourself, then you are genuine. Blase was a genuine and principled person. Everyone always knew where he was coming from because he had no hidden agenda.

Help others by sharing your wealth—money, knowledge, time

You do not need to be wealthy to help others. We all have something to contribute to help our fellow man. Volunteer at your church, be a

Big Brother, join the Peace Corps, share some time with a lonely person, help a neighbor. If you do have money, share it with those in need, and it will come back to you a hundredfold.

Live each day as if it was your last

We are only on this Earth for a short period of time. In the case of Blase, he lived sixty years, seven months, and two days. I'm guessing, however, it would have probably taken most of us ninety years to accomplish what he did in his lifetime. He certainly tried to make each new day the best day of his life, although it's hard to imagine how tough it must have been in those last few weeks. Nonetheless, he never wavered in his attempt to beat cancer.

Pray

Prayer was a significant part of Blase's life. He prayed to God to help him be a good person, to share his blessings and good fortune, and to help others. When he needed prayers the most, he received them, and God heard all the prayers from those who knew him and loved him. I believe it was prayer that kept him going for so long.

Believe in miracles

I believe miracles happen all the time. I believe every time a child is born, we experience a miracle. I'm sure many of us have met people who have either personally experienced or know of people who experienced miraculous events in their lives. I believe Blase did receive numerous miracles, or at a minimum, some kind of divine or spiritual support throughout his ordeal with cancer. In fact, Blase experienced four miracles in the form of his beautiful grandchildren, all of whom were born after his cancer was discovered. Immediately after his first operation on September 12, 2001, after seeing the size of the tumor on Blase's lung, the doctor said he was surprised it had not spread everywhere. This was eight months before Cecilia, his first grandchild, was born. Many of us believe it was miraculous that Blase showed the strength and grace to survive as long as he did and to handle his suffering in such an inspiring way.

On May 17, 2008, the circle of life continued for Kevin, Kate, and the entire Cooke family when little Ethan Blase Cooke was born. Although Blase never had the opportunity to hold Ethan in his arms, I'm sure a part of his spirit will be with Ethan forever.

Dawn and Ethan Blase Cooke, May 2008

***

The Thought for the Day below was sent out by Blase on February 23, 2006. It was the last Thought for the Day he ever sent. At that time, his ability to walk had deteriorated to the point where he needed a walker to get around, and he was just a few weeks away from enduring a serious spinal operation. I'm wondering how he found the strength to wake up that morning, let alone read the email from our cousin, Cathy, and then think about sharing it with others. This single gesture illustrates how he always thought about helping others, even as he was going through one of the toughest periods in his life. Even on that particular day, he wanted to share his excitement for life with other people. Somehow he was going to convince himself that in spite of all the suffering and difficulty he would endure that day, he was going to try to make it the best day of his life. Now that I think about it, perhaps October 2, 2007, was, in fact, the best day of his life ever because it was the day he was reunited with his God, his mom, and his everlasting family in Heaven.

Memorandum

To: All Employees

From: Blase Cooke

Re: THOUGHT FOR THE DAY

Today, when I awoke, I suddenly realized that this is the best day of my life, ever. There were times when I wondered if I would make it to today, but I did! And because I did, I'm going to celebrate!

Today, I'm going to celebrate what an unbelievable life I have had so far: the accomplishments, the many blessings, and yes, even the hardships because they have served to make me stronger. I will go through this day with my head held high and a happy heart. I will marvel at God's seemingly simple gifts: the morning dew, the sun, the clouds, the trees. Today, none of these miraculous creations will escape my notice.

Today, I will share my excitement for life with other people. I'll make someone smile. I'll go out of my way to perform an unexpected act of kindness for someone I don't even know. Today, I'll give a sincere compliment to someone who seems down. I'll tell a child how special he is, and I'll tell someone I love just how deeply I care for them and how much they mean to me.

Today is the day I quit worrying about what I don't have and start being grateful for all the wonderful things God has already given me. I'll remember that to worry is just a waste of time because my faith in God and His divine plan ensures everything will be just fine.

My Brother, My Keeper

And tonight, before I go to bed, I'll go outside and raise my eyes to the heavens. I will stand in awe at the beauty of the stars and the moon, and I will praise God for these magnificent treasures.

As the day ends and I lay my head down on my pillow, I will thank the Almighty for the best day of my life. And I will sleep the sleep of a contented child, excited with expectation because I know tomorrow is going to be the best day of my life, ever!

Thanks to Cathy Walsh for sending this to me.

Memories of Blase

I mentioned in the preface that I sent out an email soliciting Blase's family, friends, and coworkers to send me their stories about how Blase inspired them. A number of these were incorporated throughout the previous chapters. Below are some beautiful thoughts, comments, and stories I received that will help complete this story. I hope you enjoy these as well.

- *In the short time he had with his grandchildren, Blase was able to build a bond with them that will be in their hearts forever.*

- *One time, I hand-wrote him a letter and sent it to him in care of Harkins. A few days later, I received a handwritten response from him in the mail. Many times we wrote discussing our families and the Lord. I am a born-again Christian and Blase and I connected there. I thought, a multi-millionaire who is a professed Christian, and meets and talks to his employees on a personal basis, I have really found a good place to work. The owner of the company started as a laborer and worked his way up to owning the company. The American dream. Blase lived it, and didn't lose his respect for the working people in the company. Blase Cooke will always be an inspiration to me and will always be a part of my life. I hope these memories are as important to you as they are to me. I'm fifty-eight years old and in all my years in construction, I have never met another man like Blase.*

- *I have always thought of myself as a caring person, but Blase made me realize how much it truly means to others to offer words of hope and encouragement, and know that someone is praying for you. I never realized the impact of that until he did that for me. It may seem like nothing to some people, but I will never, ever forget it. I have given what I could to others this*

239

year when the opportunity presented itself, whether it be money or prayers or things they might need for their home, and every time I do, I say, "This is because Blase would have done the same thing." He has left a legacy in my mind; I want to help everyone I come in contact with now. Though I know I can't help them all, it is a wonderful feeling to try, and Blase gave that to me. Hopefully I will touch someone by trying to be more like him and they can "pay it forward" as well.

- *As a Catholic, my faith has wavered over the years in personal crisis; however, Blase's faith was ever strong and his example helped me through some bad times and renewed my Catholic faith. I see Blase's leadership and guidance of Harkins and his enduring religious belief as one of the strengths of this company and its employees. Blase lived his life as an example for all of us to follow. I personally found strength in that.*

- *When I got drafted in early 1969, I was scared to death. I was told and had read that an overwhelming percentage of draftees would go right into the infantry and then directly into combat in Vietnam. I forget exactly where, but I ran into Blase, and he told me to request assignment to MP school. Blase, as you know, was an MP and he told me they needed qualified MP school applicants and that, even though I may end up in Vietnam, I probably would not see actual combat duty. He was 110% accurate in his advice. Most of my basic training buddies were assigned to combat infantry school. I volunteered for MP school, scored high in the necessary tests, and became an MP. I did end up in Vietnam, but as a military policeman in the relatively safe areas of Long Binh and Saigon. In almost every sense of the phrase, I honestly feel Blase saved my life with his advice. Even if I had survived the actual combat in 'Nam, I shudder to think of the nightmares I would have returned with.*

My Brother, My Keeper

- *In the summer of 1999, I went to Blase to ask a favor. At the time, I was running a youth group in my home parish and we had learned about an upcoming World Youth Day celebration in Santiago, Chile that fall. I had saved money for an airplane ticket, but was short on vacation time. I asked Blase if he would consider fronting me the time from next year's vacation. By the time I left his office, I had not only the time off I needed, but also a commitment from Blase to fly me down there. Through Blase's generosity, not only was I able to go, but I was able to take my daughter as well. Upon my return, I made my way to Blase's office. We had gone there to build housing for the poor. As many volunteer things go, we did not accomplish that which we set out to do. I asked Blase if I could work out a repayment plan; I felt like I should repay Harkins for the ticket. Blase made it clear that I didn't owe him or the company anything other than what I had already given; my personal best in my daily efforts on behalf of Harkins. I left Blase's office with a new sense of humility and a desire to pass along that generosity to someone in need. That moment changed me forevermore. Your brother was truly a special person who made a lasting difference in my life. I continue to aspire in whatever fashion I can to step up and share my blessings as he did so willingly.*

- *I went to see a wonderful speaker in the areas of business and life. He told me that the most wealthy people in our country have two very similar habits; one, they read, and two, they write personal notes. That weekend, I played in my member-guest golf tournament at Rolling Road Country Club, where I had an opportunity to talk to Blase and Dawn. We talked about many things, but mostly about the books we had read. Blase asked me had I ever read the book* The Greatest Salesman in the World. *I told him I hadn't, and our wonderful conversation continued. The following Monday, when I got in my office,*

I had a great idea; I'm going to write Blase Cooke a personal note telling him how much I enjoyed our conversation that day. The next day in the mail, I received a personal note from Blase along with two books, The Greatest Salesman in the World *and* The Choice *by Og Mandino. I read those books and every other book Og Mandino wrote. I send personal notes out daily and have given numerous copies of those books away to others. I've heard it said when you are gone, it is not what you say that people will remember most, it's how you made them feel. Blase made me feel very special that day and I'll never forget it.*

- *I really did not know Blase well, and only wish I had. He was blessed with the magic to use his wealth of altruism along with his monetary wealth for the greater good. We all know how rare a gift that is to possess.*

- *At a charity golf event, I am in Blase's group and he sees me struggling on my putts. He quietly tells me upon approaching the putt and getting a good read on the putt, to get firmly in my mind the visualization of the ball going into the cup. Well, it worked quite well. And I also use his philosophy of this positive mental visual thinking into my daily business and personal life. Blase continues to be a very positive force in my life!*

- *Just being around Blase was a continuing education and often a little "juicy." He was demanding at times, had no secrets or reservations in describing folks who "ticked him off," or who he felt may have altered or even "broken the rules!" You absolutely had to play fairly to be accepted by Blase. He was not only fair, but would even remind folks of the "rules" and demand they be obeyed. If you were on his team in a golfing event or tournament, you were privileged to listen to the "pep*

rally" prior to ever teeing off. "We can beat all these guys!"
he'd start. "We got a great team and we're gonna take'em all
deep! Our goal is 15 under today and 20 under tomorrow!"
Knute Rockne couldn't have done better. Blase was indeed
competitive, goal-oriented, fair, and a true American patriot.
One of his favorite sayings, "Only in America" still resonates
through my being when I have a special accomplishment or
proud moment. Blase was so thankful for all the blessings he
enjoyed. He never forgot his humble upbringing.

• *I was working at the kids' Christmas bazaar and I met a man*
who was also helping out. He was wearing a Harkins shirt. I
asked him if he worked for Harkins and he said he did. We
began to talk and I said that I assumed he knew Blase. He
could not have spoken more highly of him. He said that he was
the nicest person he knew, that he was the type of boss that
really cared about his employees, and if he asked how you
were doing, he really wanted to know. By the time we finished
speaking, I was so touched and I felt proud to say that I also
knew him. Blase will always remain in our thoughts, and
whenever I start to feel down about something, I will think of
him and remember how positive his outlook was and how
strong his faith was. I hope that I can only have half of that.

• *I must sheepishly admit that as I sat in St. Louis Church that*
Friday listening to the tributes, I cannot help but think of
other images of a Blase over the many years of our
friendship: Blase crawling under a twelve-foot table at a bar
to pour a glass of beer in my pants; Blase throwing a piña
colada out a car window onto my new pair of white pants;
Blase holding Jason on his shoulders (and the both of them
tumbling) trying to rob me of a home run in an OC homer
derby; Blase laughing like a schoolboy as we raced back to
our Disneyworld hotel rooms after our infamous "fight;"

Blase doing a cha-cha triple at Nicki's wedding and almost knocking down my elderly next-door neighbor dancing behind him; Blase sitting in a beach chair late on many an Ocean City afternoon, laughing and plotting ways we could play pranks on our friends...on and on. Rarely a day goes by that I don't think of him and the funny things that happened over the last thirty-five years with him around. The masses remember his charity (rightly so)—I remember his humor and love of a good time. God bless him!

• *As you know, we have all had our share of bets on the golf course. About twelve years ago, Blase and I made a five-dollar bet, and as you know, that is a rather nominal wager for us. After playing our hearts out side by side for eighteen holes, Blase (surprise, surprise) won the bet by the narrowest of margins. When I gave him the dirtiest, most dilapidated five-dollar bill I could find, he had me sign it as if it were a trophy. Virtually each time we played golf together after that day, he would pull that five-dollar bill out of his wallet and show it to me and we would laugh like little kids. I wouldn't be surprised if he took that bill to the grave with him. No surprise, but the first time I really had the chance to spend time with Blase was on a golf course. As luck would have it, I was playing in my first Catholic Charities Ryder Cup and my opponent was Blase. He was focused, determined, and a fierce competitor, and on that day, we struck up a friendship. I told Blase that I hoped my children would have the passion, determination, charity, competitiveness, and love of life that he exhibited. The luck of the Irish happened to be on my side for my first Ryder Cup as I beat Blase, but more importantly, I made a great friendship. At the following year's Ryder Cup, not only did I find myself on Blase's team, but my partner was Blase. We played that way until he could no longer play and we never lost as a team (more because of his play than due to mine). Blase always told me he was willing to trade other players on the team, but not me. At one of the Ryder Cup planning meetings, we were trying to figure a way to even out the teams due to Blase's team's dominance in the event. One of the other golfers in the room shared that Blase had told him that he would not trade him from his team. As more shared, we all realized that Blase had told us all that we were too critical to the team and he would never think of trading us. In his own way, he had led all of us into thinking we were the most important person on the team. He used this as a way to build team and get personal commitment to strive to play our best for him. A number of us had a good laugh at how he had us thinking it was due to our ability and criticality to the team. As usual, Blase was way ahead of us and got his desired outcome. I always looked forward to seeing him and the way he lit up a room. I think of him often with a smile on my face for my good fortune in having spent the time with him.*

- *The story of Blase skiing at Wisp Resort occurred many years ago with their friends, Burt and Elaine. We stayed in a small A-frame house, and it was one of the coldest times I can ever remember in Maryland. None of us had ever skied, so we all went to the Wisp ski shop to rent skis. Upon returning to the A-frame, we realized we had better try on our equipment and have a trial run at skiing. At that time there was snow in the driveway. You should have seen Elaine and Blase trying to turn around in the driveway with six-foot skis. Elaine and Blase got tangled and each one was giving instructions to the other on how to get untangled. It was a funny scene. After our trial run we decided to try night skiing. Blase and I went to the bunny slope and went up and down a few times. On one occasion, I went down first and was standing at the bottom of the slope talking to some lady, congratulating each other on a successful run when I looked up and who do I see but Blase coming down the slope, obviously out of control heading right for us. The young lady saw Blase and could only mutter, "Oh, shit!" Next thing we knew, there was a total wipeout with Blase laying at our feet looking up. The young lady looked at Blase lying at our feet and said, "Thank you." Blase just looked up and in typical Blase humor said, "Lady, I had nothing to do with it."*

- *About six months after Blase passed, I played in a match play golf tournament. I had to make an important putt (no lie) and I said "Blase, please help me," and I swear, a white butterfly landed on my ball. I went to putt and the butterfly followed the ball right to the hole flying above my ball. I looked at the opponent and said that butterfly was Blase.*

Recommended Readings

Book	Author (s)
Benedict's Way: An Ancient Monk's Insights for a Balanced Life Loyola Press, 2000	Lonni Collins Pratt and Father Daniel Homan, OSB
Management Techniques from the Best Damn Ship in the Navy, It's Your Ship Warner Books, 2002	Captain D. Michael Abrashoff
Big Russ and Me Hyperion, 2004	Tim Russert
Tuesdays with Morrie (And Others) Random House, 1997	Mitch Albom
It's Not About the Bike: My Journey Back to Life G. P. Putnam's Sons (Penguin Putnam, Inc.), 2000	Lance Armstrong, Sally Jenkins
The Greatest Salesman in the World (And Others) Bantam Books, 1968	Og Mandino
Final Rounds Bantam, 1996	James Dodson
Swim with the Sharks Ballantine, 1990	Harvey McKay

The Leader in You
Pocket Books, 1995

Dale Carnegie

Golf Is Not a Game of Perfect
Simon & Schuster, 1995

Dr. Bob Rotella

The Magic of Thinking Big
Simon & Schuster, 1987

David J. Schwartz

Season of Life
Simon & Schuster, 2003

Jeffrey Marx

In Search of Excellence
Warner Books, 2004

Thomas J. Peters

Crossing the Threshold of Hope
(And Others)
Alfred A. Knopf, Inc., 1994

Pope John Paul II

The Power of Positive Thinking
Fireside, 1993

Dr. Norman Vincent Peale

Think and Grow Rich
Penguin Group, 2005

Napoleon Hill

A Simple Path
Random House, 1995

Mother Theresa

The Greatest Generation
Random House, 1998

Tom Brokaw

*The Seven Habits of Highly
Successful People*
Fireside, 1990

Dr. Stephen Covey

Motivational Speakers

Wayne Dyer

Roy Firestone

Ed Foreman

Og Mandino

Earl Nightingale

Brian Tracy

Denis Waitley

Zig Ziglar

About the Author

Phil Cooke is a consultant who provides sales and marketing services to high technology companies. He and his wife, Wanda, live in Oak Hill, Virginia, just outside of Washington, DC.

About the Website: www.mybrothermykeeper.com

I have worked in the high-tech industry for most of my adult life, although I certainly do not consider myself a "techie." Fortunately for me, my children are very tech savvy. My son, Matthew, recently launched his second high-tech company and my daughters, Nicol and Megan, have been involved with interactive advertising, helping clients enhance their web presence, so launching a website seemed like the natural thing to do. I seized the opportunity to solicit their creative expertise to help make this happen. Not only are they exceptional at what they do, but the price was right. On a serious note, I want to gratefully acknowledge my children for exceeding all my expectations, not only with the website, but for just about everything they have done in their lives. They have given Wanda and me more joy and happiness then they could imagine, and we thank God every day for our children, their spouses, and our five incredible grandchildren.

We decided to build this website for a number of reasons, not the least of which was to solicit stories about the heroes and inspirational people in your lives. When I first decided to chronicle Blase's life, I wasn't sure of the ultimate outcome. Thanks to a number of wonderful folks who contributed to this effort, we were able to create a fuller picture of Blase's accomplishments throughout all aspects of his life and publish this book. I know there are many unsung heroes whose inspirational stories should be told, and with your help, I hope we will be able to share many more of them through our website. Please visit and contribute a story about the person who has made a significant difference in your life.

We also intend to provide inspirational thoughts for the day in our quest to continue the tradition that Blase began. You can help us by contributing in this area as well. Finally, we plan to offer links to other inspirational websites we discover that might help each of us help others throughout our journeys in life.